Revolutions
REVISITED

Ralph Lerner

Revolutions

The University of North Carolina Press *Chapel Hill & London*

REVISITED

Two Faces of the Politics of Enlightenment

© 1994 The University of
North Carolina Press

Manufactured in the United States of America

The paper in this book meets the guidelines for
permanence and durability of the Committee on
Production Guidelines for Book Longevity of the
Council on Library Resources.

Library of Congress Cataloging-in-Publication Data
Lerner, Ralph.
Revolutions revisited : two faces of the politics of
enlightenment / by Ralph Lerner.
p.   cm.
Includes bibliographical references and index.
ISBN 0-8078-2136-5 (cloth : alk. paper)
1. Political science—United States—History.
2. Enlightenment—United States.
3. Enlightenment.   I. Title.
JA84.U5L387   1994
320.5'0973—dc20   93-36438
                        CIP

98   97   96   95   94   5   4   3   2   1

'Tis not enough your Counsel still be *true,*

Blunt Truths more Mischief than *nice Falshoods* do;

Men must be *taught* as if you taught them *not*;

And Things *unknown* propos'd as Things *forgot.*

—Alexander Pope, *An Essay on Criticism*

Contents

Preface

In politics as in love, words are inseparable from the thoughts they stir and expectations they rouse. "Enlighten" promises exposure, unveiling, clarity. All the more so "enlightenment," a movement devoted to plainly telling the truth. This is emphatically the case with modern enlighteners, who have shed the caution or modesty that marked their predecessors and who fairly trumpet expectations. Their promise to free a humanity enslaved to false fears and false hopes alerts us to the political consequences of such a project. But it may also distract us from attending to the politics of the enlightenment process itself. For truth to tell, enlightenment is no simple matter of truth-telling.

Those enlighteners whose enthusiasm had not dulled their shrewdness knew that long ago. The sudden and rough bustling-in of a new truth has never been welcome to all. Enlightenment requires politics if only because enlightenment is the end-point of the process, not its beginning. Given the contrariety of human beings' opinions and the divergence of their interests, the truth that would make us free can have no easy time of it.

Far from ignoring such obstacles to popular enlightenment, early modern leaders and abettors of the movement sought to take them head-on. Yet though the end in view was clear, even simple, the means for bringing it about were anything but plain and direct. A revolution had first to be made—in institutions, thinking, and expectations. Further, the revolution that would produce enlightenment must thereafter and repeatedly be explained and defended against overt enemies without and covert enemies within. Paradoxically, a movement in the name of plain speaking could not rely on blunt instruments; shouting loudly that the emperor was naked was not enough. To succeed, the politics of enlightenment must be a politics of finesse.

The reasons for this are not far to seek, although they come to sight more readily among the Americans of the eighteenth century than among their French contemporaries. The former, mere provincials but long in practical political experience, had the clearer view of the limits of enlightenment premises and principles. If some of them thought that even the most rational government would not find it a superfluous advantage to have the prejudices of the community on its side, that bespoke no failure of nerve. Their French counterparts, long in sophistication but for the most part politically mere novices and voyeurs, lacked such prudence. Preoccupied with the specter of enemies of enlightenment, they were ill-prepared to recognize foes among apparent friends.

The following pages explore how some politically minded men, notable alike for their sobriety and clarity, sought to win over the thoughts and actions of their own and succeeding generations. Those efforts illumine in striking ways the truth of a deeply considered observation by Alexis de Tocqueville: the hatred that free individuals (or those who deserve to be free) harbor for absolute power is born simultaneously of a well-thought-out idea and an instinctive feeling. The politics of enlightenment consists precisely in conveying that idea and in engaging that feeling in others.

In Part 1 of this book the mood is primarily prospective and frankly reconstructive. How do those who most emphatically have a revolution in mind, a revolution that would constitute a deep change in how one thinks about the world and one's place in it, address their public so as to help effect that inner transformation? In each case they focus their attention on means of securing a qualitative improvement in the aspirations and achievements of the people at large.

Pride of place here is given to Benjamin Franklin, the "Dr. Janus" of the initial chapter, and specifically to his "Silence Dogood" essays. Although juvenile productions, they already display the deft touch, irony, wicked humor, and broad outlines of his mature politics. The attacks on pretension in high places and low, on aristocratic or pseudoaristocratic presumptuousness, on modes of thinking that conceal or ignore the play of interest and vanity and utility in everyday life: these and similar great Franklinian themes are developed with gusto by the youthful writer. My discussion considers Franklin's writing and argumentation in these essays as modes of furthering individual and social enlightenment.

The second chapter attempts to locate America and the Americans in the Enlightenment as a whole. Enlighteners on both sides of the Atlantic agreed on much, but their differences in tone and substance are equally striking. Then too, America played a complex role as an object of scrutiny, leading Europeans sometimes to expressions of wonder, sometimes to contempt, and sometimes to admiration and emulation. Enlightened Americans' view of Europe was also complicated by mixed feelings of awe, envy, and disgust. Those differences grew out of, even as they manifested themselves in, different modes of arguing and different practical political expectations.

This first, forward-facing section of the book ends with an intergenerational comparison. Long-lived American enlighteners had the opportunity and inclination to reflect on their revolutionary handiwork and to consider the future of the new nation they had helped found. The stance of the successors resembled that of their elders. Among the most thoughtful in each generation one finds a measured regard for their respective past along with a professed commitment to surpass it. The program of enlightenment had not yet run its course.

In Part 2 the mood is primarily retrospective, and the political program is presented as restorative. Responding to the profound political, constitutional, and social divisions that shook late-eighteenth-century Britain and mid-nineteenth-century America and France, some political actors saw fit to call for a reexamination of their respective nations' revolutionary heritage. This was no merely tactical demand and was propelled by more than a desire for rhetorical advantage over partisan opponents. Rather, three of those figures who were most insistent and successful in focusing public attention on "our revolution" each held the recovery and proper understanding of his nation's past to be a matter of life or death for his constitutional regime's survival and integrity. The implications for future actions were thus to be deduced from an earlier revolutionary generation's words and deeds; yet it is also true that each of these recoveries of the past significantly reworked the very tradition it purported to defend.

What makes Edmund Burke, Abraham Lincoln, and Alexis de Tocqueville especially fitting objects of study in this respect is not some shared stance toward enlightenment thinking or toward the Enlightenment as a movement. (If anything, their views are mixed and heterogeneous.) Rather, it is their clear-sighted political understanding—of the crisis of their times, of the need to make their public face it squarely, and above all of the skill to bring about that necessary confrontation. Their recourse to history was a way of calling a people to their senses through appeals to memory, reason, passion, and pride. Drawing on dialectical and rhetorical arguments, these statesmen dared at one and the same time to rouse an indifferent or hostile public and to make their problematic account appear unexceptionable, almost self-evident. Doing this took not only courage but also art. I conclude that the kind of discourse these political figures engaged in entitles them to be regarded as masters of a political art once closely analyzed by Plato and his medieval students but now nearly forgotten. These moderns show the continuing necessity for a kind of speech that seeks to persuade voters today and predispose minds for tomorrow, all the while inching their public toward thoughtfulness. Theirs might be said to be enlightenment's other face.

((   ))

Two of these chapters have previously been published in slightly different versions. "Dr. Janus" first appeared in *Reappraising Benjamin Franklin: A Bicentennial Perspective*, edited by J. A. Leo Lemay (Newark: University of Delaware Press, 1993; © 1993 Associated University Presses, Inc.), 415–24. "A Dialogue of Fathers and Sons" was originally part of a longer essay, "Facing Up to the Founding," which appeared in *To Form a More Perfect Union: The Critical Ideas of the Constitution*, edited by Herman Belz, Ronald Hoffman, and Peter J. Albert (Charlottesville: published for the United States Capitol Historical Society by the University Press of Virginia, 1992), 250–71, used with permission from the University Press of Virginia. I thank these editors and publishers for their kind permission to reprint. The studies that constitute Part 2 of this volume grew out of an invitation to address the Institut Raymond Aron at the École des Hautes Études en Sciences Sociales in Paris in May 1992. I am grateful to my colleague François Furet for arranging that occasion. Thomas S. Schrock has borne with patience and good nature as I drew on his acuity and plainspoken judgment. My debts to him have only compounded over the years.

I

Looking Forward

1

Dr. Janus

"'But what god am I to say thou art, Janus of double shape?' asks Ovid in the *Fasti* (1.89).[1] To this question the god, appearing in his proper person, gives no clear reply in the passage which follows. So the learned of every generation continue with high courage to supplement his remarks as

---

1. *Quem tamen esse deum te dicam, Iane biformis?* Taking a cue from Benjamin Franklin, I supply the original Latin: "Gentle Readers, we design never to let a Paper pass without a Latin Motto if we can possibly pick one up, which carries a Charm in it to the Vulgar, and the learned admire the pleasure of Construing." Franklin, "The Printer to the Reader," 11 Feb. 1723, in *The Papers of Benjamin Franklin*, edited by Leonard W. Labaree et al., 29 vols. to date (New Haven: Yale University Press, 1959–), 1:50 (hereafter cited as *Papers*).

best they can."[2] These lines with which a modern classicist begins her study of the Roman god might serve as well for our point of departure and our apology. For of our Janus too—Benjamin Franklin—it may be said that for all his replies to the query, "Who are you?," much remains unanswered, much remains to be puzzled over. This man of many masks and voices, our native master of satire and hoax, of parable and bagatelle, preserves to himself a core that defies simple explanation even while inviting it. How fitting and prescient, then, that the young apprentice, on taking nominal charge of his fugitive brother's newspaper, *The New-England Courant*, adopts as his persona "good Old Janus the Couranteer." Rather than name the various friends who were temporarily assuming James Franklin's responsibilities in 1723, young Ben dons instead a concealing mask. He presents to the curious public the person of "an Inhabitant of this Town of Boston, [one] whom we honour as a Doctor in the Chair, or a perpetual Dictator." Said Janus is of course a man of double face and hence of double view, the best qualified of local folk for "an *Observator*, being a Man of such remarkable *Opticks*, as to look two ways at once." But aside from his distinctive visage and the announcement that he is "a chearly Christian," "a mortal Hater of Nonsense, Foppery, Formality, and endless Ceremony,"[3] we know little enough about this Couranteer.

Such reticence sets Janus quite apart from another of Franklin's memorable personae, that no-nonsense viewer of the social landscape, Silence Dogood. When she first appears in print, Mistress Dogood acknowledges and, so to speak, gratifies the curiosity that makes the modern reading public peek behind the name, behind the facade. They insist on knowing who or what the author is before delivering their

2. Louise Adams Holland, *Janus and the Bridge*, American Academy in Rome Papers and Monographs, no. 21 (Rome: American Academy in Rome, 1961), 3.

3. Franklin, "The Printer to the Reader," *Papers* 1:48–50.

judgment of whatever they have read. Mistress Dogood accordingly launches into an account of her past life and present condition, a narrative at once hilarious, racy, fanciful, and deft.[4] In both telling us about herself and demonstrating her character through her choice of matter and manner, this not-so-humble "Humble Servant" persuades us that she indeed has no intention of wrapping her talent in a napkin. Because she is not at all shy in pronouncing her judgments and principles, she stirs something that rouses us from passivity. In reading her account, we are invited to consider Silence Dogood herself and to distinguish her from her sixteen-year-old creator. In some cases we may well press on to ponder how Franklin looks at us, even as we busily observe his merry widow, now "sharp and satyrical, then (to mollify that) . . . sober and religious."[5] Precisely because these masks and artifices are so close to the surface of our thoughts, we can laugh freely with her without risk of losing the critical distance we need to take her measure and draw our own conclusions. With deceptive ease Franklin is able to use her sauciness and independence of mind to lead us toward comparable independence. From this perspective Franklin's larger message may consist more in the example of Silence Dogood than in the particulars of her critiques (telling as those public scoldings are). She mirrors what we might yet become.

Franklin is by no means loath to teach, but he is acutely aware of the attendant pitfalls. He knows that most people do not cotton to heavy-handed moralizing, let alone act on prescribed sound opinions.[6] He chooses instead to win us

4. Franklin, "Silence Dogood," nos. 1 and 2, 2 and 16 Apr. 1722, *Papers* 1:9–13.

5. Ibid., no. 3, 30 Apr. 1722, *Papers* 1:14.

6. Accordingly I would read "The Way to Wealth," Father Abraham's crushingly tedious and one-sided invocation of great sayings from *Poor Richard's Almanack*, as having less to do with the maxims themselves than with the reaction of the crowd to the old gentle-

over to a way of thinking, confident that its mode and themes will effect a cumulative substantive change. It is this end that Franklin's own persistent two-facedness is meant to foster and serve. He takes aim squarely at the human inclination to defer to authority, be it of the great or of the many. He means to overcome our bent for aping the opinions and manners of others and seeking out models who might spare us the pains of thinking for ourselves. Franklin, like Silence Dogood, holds to the view that the best way of showing our love for religion and country is to emphatically counter this tendency toward thoughtless deference wherever it appears, whether in ourselves or in others. By "undeceiving the Deceived," Silence Dogood acts so as to enable all but the most incorrigibly gullible to look at this world with their own eyes, to identify their own interests, and to assess their own worth ("none but your great Self can tell your Own").[7] Franklin's projection of many masks is thus more than a product of his fertile, restless imagination. His many faces, and not least that presented in his memoirs, may serve to warn or encourage. But it is, I think, a misreading to assume that they are meant as simple prescriptions for others. Rather, Franklin uses his art to emphasize the madcap or defective or comical side of these characters. In so doing he works against the straightforward or slavish imitation of any given model and hence against dependence as such. Were we to suspend our disbelief and join in the spirit of the fiction, we should hardly

---

man's harangue: "The People heard it, and approved the Doctrine, and immediately practised the contrary, just as if it had been a common Sermon." Franklin, Preface to *Poor Richard Improved* (1758), *Papers* 7:350.

7. Franklin, "Silence Dogood," no. 9, 23 July 1722, *Papers* 1:31; Franklin, "A Panegyrick," appended to "Silence Dogood," no. 7, 25 June 1722, in Benjamin Franklin, *Writings*, edited by J. A. Leo Lemay (New York: Library of America, 1987), 23 (hereafter cited as *Writings*).

do so out of a desire to actually reshape our lives after Silence Dogood or Polly Baker or even the young apprentice portrayed in the *Autobiography.* When we permit ourselves to be taken in, it is rather by the spectacle of a quite imperfect being struggling to find its own mind and voice and will. It is not farfetched to claim that, for Franklin, a little lie may help in grasping a large truth.

Franklin's acts and writings bear strong witness to this belief. Consider, to begin with, that helpful precept by which Franklin, in his catalogue of the virtues, expresses the meaning he gives to the term "Sincerity." It is, of course, easier to be sincere if one already enjoys some measure of "Affluence & Independance." By having the means to be one's own man, one may more readily think innocently and justly and speak accordingly. But equally evident from this explanatory precept—"Use no hurtful Deceit"—is that "Sincerity" does not preclude deceit as such.[8] Franklin means more than to allow for those little white lies we are pleased to call "tact." For as his whole life demonstrates and as his avowed method encourages us to conclude, the promotion of good works toward one's fellows in fact requires the use of artifice and concealment. It is by indirection and subterfuge that human beings are first brought to the good they desire but that they for the most part cannot autonomously and forthrightly bring themselves to attain. Consider the Junto, Franklin's club for young men big with projects for private and public improvement. One need only recall the secrecy with which its members formed subordinate cells and simulated the independent discovery of points of view with an eye to

8. Franklin, *Autobiography,* in *Writings,* 1385–86. Yet affluence is neither the necessary nor a sufficient condition for attaining "Consciousness of [one's] own innate Worth." Franklin's rough-hewn, country Cato is equally free of false humility and unbecoming assurance; see Franklin, "The Busy-Body," no. 3, 18 Feb. 1729, *Papers* 1:119–20.

"influencing the public Opinion on particular Occasions." Here was a classic instance of beneficent deceit.[9]

Our Janus is never more candid than when speaking of dissimulation as he does, for example, in his essay "On Simplicity." Like Lord Bacon, his cited authority in bad-mouthing cunning, Franklin understands that "it asks a strong Wit and a strong Heart, to know when to tell Truth and to do it."[10] By and large, simplicity seems best. So it was at least in the beginning. For even though primordial men were not without their cunning devices, these were employed in trapping and taming the beasts, not one another. Here lies the difference between the use and abuse of cunning. By modern times, Franklin explains, "those little Basenesses" have come to be reckoned among "the necessary Arts and Knowledges of Life." No longer matter for private misgiving or public embarrassment, modern knavery has achieved a free field of action and leaves its mark on every aspect of life. Franklin heightens his attack by insisting that candor was the distinctive charm of the ancient authors. In their very telling of "the frank and open Characters of the Heroes they cele-

9. Franklin, *Autobiography,* in *Writings,* 1402–3. Thus, for example, Franklin's plan for reforming the City Watch: "This Idea being approv'd by the Junto, was communicated to the other Clubs, but as arising in each of them." Ibid., 1405. It is not only the public but the proposers as well who are managed. None of this, however, is to suggest that Franklin's method is reducible simply to subterfuge and manipulation. The Junto and its offshoots had open agenda and curricula. See Franklin, "Standing Queries for the Junto" and "Proposals and Queries to be Asked the Junto," ca. 1732, *Papers* 1:256–64.

10. Franklin, "On Simplicity," 13 Apr. 1732, *Writings,* 182. The case for attributing this essay in the *Pennsylvania Gazette* to Franklin's pen is made in J. A. Leo Lemay, *The Canon of Benjamin Franklin 1722–1776: New Attributions and Reconsiderations* (Newark: University of Delaware Press, 1986), 60–62. The passage quoted in the text is part of Franklin's conflation of the openings of Bacon's essays "Of Simulation and Dissimulation" (no. 6) and "Of Cunning" (no. 22).

brate," the old Greeks and Romans gravitated to that "just and beautiful Stile and Sentiment" which befitted those heroic actions and manners. Franklin leaves the reader to infer that in our times such writing would be quite as out of place and unfashionable as such behavior.[11]

Whatever else might be said of this account, it does seem simplistic. But like Bacon's *Essays*, this work makes a series of rapid reversals, twisting the argument this way and that and provoking the reader to further, deeper thoughts. Almost immediately it becomes clear that modern corruption is by no means total. We need only leave town to once again breathe wholesome air. Metropolitan double-dealing stands in sharp contrast to rural candor, "the simple and unaffected Dialogues of uncorrupted Peasants."[12] Further, even in the innermost corridors of power some rare types may be found, men of the truest genius and highest characters in the conduct of the world, who yet possess simplicity in the highest degree. These might be thought of as men of genuine (as distinguished from false or foolish) policy. "They are Pretenders only, to Policy and Business, who have recourse to Cunning, and the little Chicaneries thereof." But Franklin is not content to settle for this. He goes on to press the conclusions that "wise Men cannot help being honest"; that simplicity is not only natural, but the highest beauty of nature and the object of excellence in the arts; that "nothing is so tiresome to one's self, as well as so odious to others, as

11. Franklin, "On Simplicity," 13 Apr. 1732, *Writings*, 181–82. Nonetheless, what *young* Ben found charming and irresistible about "Xenophon's Memorable Things of Socrates" was a method of artfully entrapping one's opponent in debate; see Franklin, *Autobiography*, in *Writings*, 1321.

12. Franklin, "On Simplicity," *Writings*, 182. This, too, is overdrawn. Silence Dogood, a country girl, confesses (to her shame) to the same kind of pride and desire for overweening superiority as the townsfolk she berates. Franklin, "Silence Dogood," no. 6, 11 June 1722, *Papers* 1:21.

Disguise and Affectation." As a purely personal vice, cunning is bad enough; but when practiced in "free and mixed Assemblies" it is downright inconvenient! "A cunning Man," Franklin concludes, "is obliged to hunt his Game alone."[13]

Even those readers who are persuaded by such arguments might draw up short on encountering the penultimate paragraph of Franklin's essay on simplicity. For far from urging us to clasp the simple, the plainspoken, and the unfashionable to our bosoms, Franklin urges caution in assessing these human types. There is such a thing as a mask of simplicity, an affectation of "Quaintness of Habit, or Oddness of Behaviour" far removed from the genuine article. How, then, would Franklin have us test and detect such pretensions? How can we recognize that plainness and integrity of mind which truly fits people for great and honest actions? The essay's answer appears to be that it is enough to be forewarned: knavery and pretense will out. "No Mask ever hid it self."[14]

What an extraordinary conclusion for this man of many masks to promote! In one respect it is tantamount to asserting that Franklin is indifferent to the notoriety he enjoys as a masquerader. The fact that he is known at times to pretend to be what he is not, the fact that he conceals himself, presumably does not implicate his basic integrity and simplicity because *he* knows he always means well. That self-knowledge leads him to open expressions of self-concealment and self-assertion. Richard Saunders mocks his envious fellow philomaths and almanac-makers: "*Who knows him?* they cry: *Where does he live?*—But what is that to them? If I delight in a private Life, have they any Right to drag me out of my Retirement? I have good Reasons for concealing the Place of my Abode."[15]

13. Franklin, "On Simplicity," *Writings*, 182–83.
14. Ibid., 183–84.
15. Franklin, Preface to *Poor Richard's Almanack* (1742), *Papers* 2:332.

Franklin, like Poor Richard, like Janus himself, has his reasons for not divulging all. Those reasons guide his strategy and inform his method, but he thinks they are basically his business, not ours. Franklin means to free us from a host of unexamined assumptions with a view to warding off a host of wretched consequences. To do this he presents a certain face to the world. That face mocks all forms of nonsense, foppery, and pretense. It works against the kinds of self-indulgence that invite personal ruin and domineering by others or, alternatively, the exercise of tyrannical impulses through the domination of others. It works as well against the kinds of selflessness that make one less capable of dealing with the world as it is. Rather than promote exemplary lives for others to vainly ape, Franklin creates models who themselves eschew imitation and who therefore encourage us to think and act likewise. By presenting them warts and all, Franklin avoids substituting one imaginary model of perfection for another. Unlike the clergy they delight in lampooning, Franklin's masked figures send the message "do as I do, not as I say." Thus when Silence Dogood is no longer heard from, when she at long last does keep silence, her correspondent and avid reader shows that he has not quite taken her lessons to heart. If she is still among the living, let her proceed as usual, Hugo Grim writes; "or if not, let us know it, that some other hand may take up your Pen."[16] But Mr. Grim's wish is not to be fulfilled, at least not by Ms. Dogood. For if she is intent on anything, it is to refrain from creating yet another figure of authority, another doctrine that saps the desire for individual self-reliance. Silence will keep her peace, and in that silence everyone may now begin thinking and acting for himself or herself. Everyone may now observe and reprove the faults in others or in oneself without benefit of further cues from the Great Reprover. The true success of Franklin's

16. Franklin, "Hugo Grim on Silence Dogood," 3 Dec. 1722, *Writings*, 43. On this attribution to Franklin, see Lemay, *Canon*, 27–28.

platoon of cranky, unforgettable characters is that they prepare the reader's way to Franklin's positive program.

( )

That program begins by making few concessions to polite dress and no apologies at all for plain talk. In the name of sincerity, Poor Richard rejects as pretense any claim to writing an almanac out of a disinterested regard for the public good. The truth is that he is poor and that his wife's tastes run beyond his means. Franklin, in his own name, is not embarrassed to draw attention to both the public utility of his almanac and the private advantages he "reap'd" from it. He also makes a point of separating himself from those who disclaim any vanity of their own and condemn vanity in others: "I give it fair Quarter wherever I meet with it, being persuaded that it is often productive of Good to the Possessor & to others that are within his Sphere of Action."[17] Here are the rudiments of an education in self-knowledge. By learning how to recognize and accept vanity, we are better situated to govern it. Self-correction is the fruit of self-knowledge, which is perhaps only another way of saying that a candid respect for ourselves can lead to our having good reasons for being proud. As Poor Richard says, "He may well win the race that runs by himself."[18]

By spurning counsels of perfection that do violence to human nature, we avoid adding to the sum of envy and resentment in this world. Franklin would have us direct our efforts to matters that are within reach. Thus, his "Art of Virtue" is, in effect, an education in moderation and civility, a corrective to grandiose high-flying notions.[19] The original

17. Franklin, Preface to *Poor Richard's Almanack* (1733), *Papers* 1:311; Franklin, *Autobiography*, in *Writings*, 1397, 1308.

18. Franklin, *Poor Richard's Almanack* (1747), *Papers* 3:102.

19. One might surmise that Franklin's injunction to "Imitate Jesus and Socrates" is anything but moderate and civil, even as an explica-

impulse for Franklin's "bold and arduous Project of arriving at moral Perfection" stems directly from his commendable wish to live a faultless life: "I would conquer all that either Natural Inclination, Custom, or Company might lead me into. As I knew, or thought I knew, what was right and wrong, I did not see why I might not *always* do the one and avoid the other." The shock at being "surpriz'd" by one fault after another drives Franklin to devise a fail-safe method for triumphing over weakness and inattention. But that method, too, is only a qualified success. Something that "pretended to be Reason" suggested to Franklin that "such extream Nicety as I exacted of my self might be a kind of Foppery in Morals," exposing him to becoming an object of derision, envy, and hate. The ironical conclusion is vintage Dr. Janus: "a benevolent Man should allow a few Faults in himself, to keep his Friends in Countenance."[20]

At how many points might one enter into this account and find matter for speculation! A public-spirited old man tells a story of how a naive enthusiast learned a lesson about life, addressing the story to mere novices who, had they the wit to look hard, might discover they have been speaking with a crafty old sophister. It is striking that Franklin thinks it useful and perhaps needful to cast his account in this way. Without even pretending to have counted all the boxes within boxes

---

tion of "Humility." Indeed, almost everything he says about this virtue is provocative. Franklin is informed by a Quaker friend's "kindly" but insistently detailed bill of particulars that he is thought proud, even insolent. He is persuaded to add "Humility" as an afterthought to his list of virtues. Franklin affects not to know whether pride is a vice or a folly, but he knows well enough that *his* "Humility" has more show than substance. He leads us to conclude that in this pridefulness he is not alone, that (leaving self-knowledge aside) he may not differ much from his Quaker friend or from civil folk generally. Franklin, *Autobiography,* in *Writings,* 1385, 1392–94.

20. Ibid., 1383–84, 1390. Thus in confessing to his failings as respects "Order," "Chastity," and "Humility," Franklin's memoir also attests to his benevolence.

here, I am compelled to suspect that this is not mere artfulness running amok or an indulgence in sleight of hand for its own sake. Severally and together, these charming tales and complications constitute an education Franklin thinks worth administering.

Need one say that Franklin's notion of an appropriate education is hardly to be sought in "*our College*"? The bitter yet hilarious fugue played out by Silence Dogood and her reverend boarder, Clericus, makes this evident to all but Clericus himself. Keeping his nose in a book, Clericus cannot see where he walks. Blinkered by his all-too-ready acceptance of authority, blinded by certitude, self-satisfaction, and vanity, he is the very caricature and "*lively Representation*" of all that Franklin means to oppose through his lifelong masquerades. The whole charade that passes as the "Temple of Learning" is detected and overthrown by Ms. Dogood on her own, in a dream that overtakes her on a solitary walk while "still ruminating on Clericus's Discourse with much Consideration." In these matters there is no reason to defer to the pronunciamentos of others. Such deference appears in the dream as a blend of idolatry and fraud. Knowledge of what should be is accessible to any independent mind that has been schooled in commonsense observation and practiced in useful conversation.[21] But although Silence presents herself as very much her own woman, she is by no means simply self-made. Farmed out for others to raise as though she were an orphan, she soon was indeed left "as it were by my self." But this early and avid reader had the "free Use" of a small but select library, "well chose, to inform the Understanding rightly, and enable the Mind to frame great and noble Ideas." She has a character that makes her "naturally very jealous for the Rights and Liberties of my Country; and the least appearance of an Incroachment on those invaluable Priviledges, is apt to make my Blood boil exceedingly."[22] Hers is

21. Franklin, "Silence Dogood," no. 4, 14 May 1722, *Papers* 1:14–18.
22. Franklin, "Silence Dogood," no. 1, 2 Apr. 1722, *Papers* 1:10;

an upbringing that makes her especially ready to be useful to others because she already knows how to be useful to herself.

The social consequences of this education in self-respect are of abiding interest to Franklin, whatever mask he happens to have donned. Like Janus he stands at the city's gate, facing citizens within and strangers without. He has them both much in mind. They in turn associate him with new beginnings, with commerce and trade and money, with the making of treaties and the maintenance of peace.[23] There is a fullness here that exposes Father Abraham's homily in "The Way to Wealth" for the perversely lopsided production it is.[24] Thus any serious assessment of Franklin takes care to make his different voices heard.[25] It is well-known that his "Art of

---

ibid., no. 2, 16 Apr. 1722, *Papers* 1:13. These lines antedate Parliament's passage of the Sugar Act by more than forty years.

23. See the discussion in Holland, *Janus and the Bridge*, 305–6.

24. James Parton concludes that "the worst effect of the piece has been to perpetuate the opinion, that the large and liberal Franklin was a mere devotee of penny-saving prudence." Parton, *Life and Times of Benjamin Franklin*, 2 vols. (New York, 1864), 1:228. See also the judicious editorial comment on "Poor Richard Improved, 1758," in Franklin, *Papers* 7:326–27; and Patrick Sullivan, "Benjamin Franklin, The Inveterate (and Crafty) Public Instructor: Instruction on Two Levels in 'The Way to Wealth,' " *Early American Literature* 21 (1986/87): 248–59.

25. Franklin's many-sidedness is not solely an expression of his genius, as one may observe by comparing him to his contemporary Edmund Pendleton, another self-made man, the temper of whose politics much resembled Franklin's. Each deliberated carefully in presenting himself to the public he meant to persuade and lead. Each cultivated an air of amiability that much impressed his fellows. But beyond that, the great Virginian debater, whose chosen forum was the legislative hall and the courtroom, strove to gain and preserve a reputation for consistent expertness, openness, and level-headedness. Franklin, in contrast, knew he was no orator and detested disputation. He relied instead on private conversation and on the written word to reach a broader public. Those favored

Virtue," his memoirs, his maxims strewed through the twenty-six years of almanacs, all seek to connect self-respect with the helping of others. For Franklin civic life is impossible solely on the principles of a limited liability corporation. The self-interested claims of both governors and governed, of rich and poor, of the bold and the moderate, have to be tempered and accommodated. All this points to a political system that recognizes the equal claim of all members of society to enjoy the personal securities of life and liberty, regardless of the difference in their circumstances. At the same time it requires of citizens that, even while cherishing their natural right to property, they also understand that its enjoyment (beyond the mere preservation of self and offspring) can only be on civil society's terms. "He can have no right to the benefits of Society, who will not pay his Club towards the Support of it."[26]

---

means permitted—indeed invited—a degree of playfulness and indirection that could, if he so chose, mask his expertness and levelheadedness. The interaction of native character and the singularities of his situation thus led Franklin to practice his peculiar arts. Others might then discover on their own, as it were, whatever it was that he meant for them to learn. See the analysis of Pendleton in Jack P. Greene, "Character, Persona, and Authority: A Study of Alternative Styles of Political Leadership in Revolutionary Virginia," in *The Revolutionary War in the South: Power, Conflict, and Leadership; Essays in Honor of John Richard Alden*, edited by W. Robert Higgins (Durham, N.C.: Duke University Press, 1979), especially pp. 19–29; and Jack P. Greene, "The Alienation of Benjamin Franklin—British American," in *Journal of the Royal Society of Arts* 124 (1976): 52–73.

26. Franklin to Robert Morris, 25 Dec. 1783, *Writings*, 1081–82. See also Franklin's speech in the Federal Constitutional Convention on the subject of salaries, 2 June 1787, *Writings*, 1131–32; and Franklin, "Queries and Remarks respecting Alterations in the Constitution of Pennsylvania," Nov. 1789, in *The Writings of Benjamin Franklin*, edited by Albert Henry Smyth, 10 vols. (New York: Macmillan Co., 1905–7), 10:59–60.

But given the great force of the love of power and the love of money in prompting men and women to action, what effective check can there be on their attempts at self-affirmation? Something more is needed to steady tottering consciences, but without stirring the zeal that would propel humankind at one another's throats. In contemplating the inevitability of future times of public danger, Franklin (no less than John Milton) is concerned that the coming generation show itself to possess political backbone, that it act not as "poor, shaken, uncertain Reeds . . . but stedfast Pillars of the State."[27] Yet in linking habits of moderation to the pursuit of private advantage, Franklin tries to conceal from his readers the dangers inherent in the radical emancipation of the self. It is less important that they suspect the void in Franklin's heaven than that they center their thoughts on forming personal habits of industry, responsibility, and civility. Nor need they be especially mindful of the thin ice on which they skate when vanity is converted from a sharp departure from pious humility into, at worst, a genial weakness. By enlisting good works in the service of vanity, Franklin hopes to render self-control attractive. But this is at best a gamble. One may wonder whether individuals repeatedly prompted to find themselves, to assert themselves, and to serve themselves will, by and large and in the absence of anything more, find selves worthy of this devotion. Further, how well does their self-service comport with a free people's need to be respectful of others? Franklin's way out of the difficulty is to stress the dignity of self-determination and to reinforce that message by an intensive habituation in the ways of respectability. The success of his enterprise depends on respectability's not falling out of fashion.

With the near-disappearance of a God whose wonder-working providence is there for all to see, Franklin's trainees have to depend on their own good intentions, their own good

27. Franklin, "Proposals Relating to the Education of Youth in Pensilvania" (1749), *Papers* 3:413n. The passage quoted in the text is taken by Franklin from Milton's tractate *Of Education*.

works, and their concern for their own good names. What they hear from Franklin is unlikely to stir darker thoughts or deeper doubts about this human providence. Nor is what they hear from Franklin likely to make *him* more transparent to their understandings, given the complexity or remoteness of his mind.[28] Indeed, the very reasons that impel Franklin to conceal the dangers in his program in turn necessitate further concealments: his modes of storytelling, his bottomless box of masks, his deep reserve about fundamental beliefs and premises—even (as noted before) his reasons for concealing the place of his abode. That is the Franklin who remains guarded and covert. The youth who could not afford the time to attend Presbyterian services, "Sunday being my Studying-Day"; the man who delighted in the private use of leisure for chess and intimate conversations; the friend who speculated on the vast influence exerted by evangelist George White-field's preaching but who kept his thoughts to himself: these are all aspects of the Franklin who faces elsewhere—and of the Franklin who sees to it that we know it.

It was enough, more than enough, that through his masks and teaching and seven decades of acting on the public stage, Franklin succeeded in inclining all manner of men and women to strive for "Decent Plainness & manly Freedom."[29] We have little cause to complain that, having done and said so much, he left the learned of every generation to try to fill the remaining gaps as best they can.

28. Here life surpasses art. Franklin inserts between parts 1 and 2 of his memoirs two letters from friends urging him to proceed with the completion of his life story. Among the many reasons pressed by Benjamin Vaughan is this: "that you should let the world into the traits of your genuine character. . . . Considering your great age, the caution of your character, and your peculiar style of thinking, it is not likely that any one besides yourself can be sufficiently master of the facts of your life, or the intentions of your mind." Franklin, *Autobiography,* in *Writings,* 1377.

29. Ibid., 1320, 1382, 1406, 1313.

America's Place in the Enlightenment

How contrived and farfetched to speak of America's relation to the Enlightenment! For if it is *the* Enlightenment we have in mind—the assertive eighteenth-century French version of the movement—then, one must confess, differences and singularities are more apparent than shared concerns. At the least, we would be hard put to discover among the Americans much if any of the animus, frustration, and resentment that fueled and sustained the *philosophes* in their battles with state and society. The French were intent on reconstructing a very old state now clearly seen as incoherent, paralyzed, and broke. In America, however, the state was not only barely adolescent but barely visible. Preoccupations with sovereignty and the erection of an imposing public authority were hardly American obsessions.

Further, the French *philosophes* took deep offense at the

irrational or unprincipled foundations of the predominant social institutions. Their politics of reason was initially (although not exclusively) a politics of denial and negation. They thought reform or progressive change unlikely or impossible unless people were first brought to view the prevailing state of affairs as baseless, outrageous, and even laughable. Thanks to this campaign, mockery became a potent weapon in the hands of those who would make a better world. But this notion of undertaking a wholesale reconstruction of social life exceeded the dreams or desires of the most sanguine American. If independence and a separate nationality afforded a new beginning, it was after all a new beginning in a country itself quite new. Even custom posed no great barrier, for that American world of small societies was peopled with those who from the outset had meant to blaze new paths in the wilderness. In that setting, American judgments of prevailing practices, as gauged by the standard of reason, were less furious and more temperate than among the French. Living in what they regarded as already an enlightened society, American reformers chose to be unabashedly prudential.

It is no less striking that when the *philosophes* contemplated their political landscape, they did so as outsiders looking on. For the most part they were cut off from the corridors of power and separated from the world of affairs. They were and remained political voyeurs. Lacking experience and accountable to none, they were free to give full rein to their abundant wit and ingenuity. Their serious thought and earnest desires were embedded in a brilliant but insubstantial parlor game. In America, meanwhile, those who might with some latitude be called Enlighteners (if not *philosophes*) were themselves men of action, figuring among the foremost political leaders of their region. The arena in which they labored may have been confined—compared with the precincts of Versailles all scenes of American political life were petty, provincial, and drab—but the issues of governance, liberty, and order with which they wrestled were fundamental and universal. They learned by doing; their little schools provided them with an education beyond the reach or price of a Parisian salon.

Finally, one might wonder where to look for some American counterpart to the *philosophes'* preoccupation with church and religion. The bitter wars of the sixteenth century, having set large segments of the French population at one another's throats, left a lasting legacy in the Enlightenment's political program. Expulsion and eradication of Protestants had led not to a restoration of wholeness and harmony, but to a barely clandestine, seething resentment. One could hardly place one's faith in a church seen as selfishly political and economic. What spiritual power there was would be directed at opposing the religious tradition, at creating some substitute for religion stripped of its mystery if not of its passion. There was no situation like this in America. However much individuals and groups chafed under the overbearing righteousness of Presbyterians or Quakers or some other locally regnant sect, the heterogeneity of America's religious life exerted a remarkable calming effect.

Yet notwithstanding all these differences and their cumulative importance, there still remains this matter to be explained. It is arguable that the constitutions of government erected by the generation of American revolutionaries are the preeminent, perhaps the only, great lasting political achievement of Enlightenment philosophy. For all their differences, the provincials who undertook the American founding shared important aspirations with the European enlighteners. Their institution-building and political experiments were informed by those aspirations. Accordingly, we are not free to assume that the larger social consequences of those institutions were simply beyond their intentions or imaginings. We might expect, rather, that in their similarities and differences the two groups illumine some of the strengths and limits of the Enlightenment as a whole.

((   ))

What, then, is America's place in the Enlightenment? The question is as ambiguous as the many-sided facts from which it abstracts. One might wonder, whose America? Thomas Jefferson's or the Connecticut clergy's? Alexander Hamilton's or George Mason's? And whose Enlightenment? John Locke's or Beccaria's? David Hume's or Condorcet's? Nor is it obvious what one means by "place."

To be sure, America has a place insofar as it can be located within the larger movement of thought and action that took shape in Western Europe during the century or so preceding the adoption of the Constitution of the United States. That movement, for all its philosophical origins, was most emphatically driven by a political program. It took aim at the absurd pretensions of the overbearing few and at the whole political and economic system that enshrined and sustained those delusions. By projecting a steady beam of light on the shadow-play of existing social practices, the Enlighteners planned to expose the indefensible and prepare the way for its replacement by something more solid, more useful, and more just. Individuals adhering to this program differed, of course, in their degrees of impatience and resentment when viewing the existing order. Indeed, some were quite lacking in that measured calm that we have come to associate with powdered wigs. But for all their differences of temperament, these men and women of the Enlightenment were as one in proposing a new basis for society. It is not easy to assign a name for what they were all proposing—people as different as Montesquieu and Adam Smith, as John Adams and Diderot—but perhaps some such term as "generic republicanism" might do.

Republicanism so understood would be neutral, by and large, toward the office of kingship, but not toward a system of exemptions and privileges based on hereditary orders. It would respect or at least make grudging allowance for national or historic differences but focus its attention mainly on the shared qualities and aspirations of newly enlightened regimes. For such republicanism, legitimacy stems not from divine grant, not from time-honored prescription, but from the consent of citizens who have matured in their freedom. A people brought to an awareness of their interests and rights can be relied on to care for themselves and hold their trustees to account.

Here the positive program of the Enlighteners comes to sight. Clearly it was not enough to explode outmoded and outrageous presuppositions. One also had to promote a kind of common sense and reasonable self-respect among the people at large. Failing that, one would only end up substituting one form of manipulation and exploitation for another. From the standpoint of generic republicanism, a democratic lynch mob is in no way superior to a sultan's silken strangler. To free mankind from the Cleons and Caligulas of this world would require nothing less than a general diffusion of some fundamental truths and the embodying of those truths in new institutions and practices.

Even at this level of abstraction it is easy to see that America has a place in the Enlightenment. The most distinctive American voices have shaped and furthered this program, spreading the word, remolding institutions, recalling an erring or complacent people to a sense of their own significance. The catalogue of movers and shakers is familiar enough: the revolutionary activities of John Adams, beginning with his "Dissertation on the Canon and the Feudal Law"; the whole life of Thomas Jefferson, crafter of pronouncements and state papers, reviser of laws, and educational reformer; the constitution-making and constitution-guarding of James Madison; the molding of public opinion, at home and abroad, by the tireless Benjamin Franklin. Joined by the likes of Benjamin Rush and Joel Barlow, seconded in their efforts by John Quincy Adams and Albert Gallatin, these men held fast to the faith that contributed so much to the original revolutionary impulse.

Yet it is not only as an also-ran that America figures in the

Enlightenment. In ways sometimes striking, sometimes bizarre, America also served as a spur, a prod to that larger movement of thought and action of which it is a part. If Europe needed to be dissuaded from further adventures in colonialism or confirmed in a sense of its own superiority, it had only to look westward. American backwardness, even primitivism, was no accident: that much was clear to Europeans from Peter Kalm's first-hand observations of degenerating species, from Buffon's theories about the effects of climate, and from de Pauw's freewheeling extrapolations in the *Encyclopédie.*[1] Conversely, if Europe needed a model of what might yet be, or a measure of how far it had sunk, or an incentive to go and sin no more, there was America ready at hand, an example of truly heroic or mythic proportions. Sober Jesuit narratives, Chateaubriand's heady account of wild America, Crèvecoeur's rural hinterland airbrushed into mildness and prettiness, Franklin's artful road show at Passy and the salons of Paris: all helped to supply whatever a *philosophe* or a politician might demand. It was an America as you like it.

Could corrupt courtiers be brought to mind of what genuine nobility consisted in? Here was Jefferson's Indian: an orator equal to Greece's finest, an ardent warrior of truly stoic endurance, nature's own nobleman. Could world-

---

1. "Now, for reasons that were sometimes scientific, but more often political or religious or personal, or even for no reasons at all, the lordliest of the French naturalists [the Comte de Buffon], the most waspish of the propagandists [the Dutch Abbé Corneille de Pauw], . . . and with them assorted scribblers in neighboring countries, joined in a kind of conspiracy to expose [the transparent backwardness and degeneracy of] Nature and Man in the New World." Henry Steele Commager, *The Empire of Reason: How Europe Imagined and America Realized the Enlightenment* (Garden City, N.Y.: Anchor Press/Doubleday, 1977), 79. For more on this campaign and on the counterattack led by Jefferson, see the lively brief account in ibid., 79–95.

weary and depressed Europeans be inspired with the possibilities of popular self-governance? Here were American rustics with barely a cracked china cup and a coonskin cap to their names, displaying prodigies of political savoir faire, founding free states, securing liberties, even taxing themselves. The Enlighteners' America was a land of many faces, but these in turn were often enough projections of the Enlighteners' own fancy. In that sense, also, America served the Enlightenment.

Of course it was not all fancy. The relentless demythologizers of Paris may have been soft touches for some New World hokum, but in fact America did show them something new and wondrous. Possibilities, abstractly considered, gain great force when one can point to them as actualities. A small people somehow or other had outlasted and sometimes outfought the preeminent military power of the age. A thinly scattered populace at the edge of the world had found ways of collecting their political energy and will and now gave every sign of meaning to become a nation. A land of small farmers was displaying commercial habits and single-mindedness worthy of an Amsterdam countinghouse. In most respects America was still promises, but ever-accumulating pieces of evidence testified to the viability of much of what the Enlightenment cherished and sought. Here, too, America had its place.

Then there is yet another way in which to place America in the Enlightenment. With its program for political action, that European movement drew on a whole series of philosophic premises and commitments. In this respect America was more than a passive party, receiving and reflecting what had emanated from others. For to paraphrase Alexis de Tocqueville, the Americans were natural Cartesians—without ever having had to crack the covers of his books. In ways that are not altogether clear, the American people as a whole absorbed and adopted from Britain or independently discovered some leading features of Enlightenment thinking. By making these their own in a situation where they were left largely to themselves, the Americans also transformed these philosophic premises and commitments. Sometimes they rendered them sharper and more radical; sometimes they mitigated or blurred their theoretical simplicity in the course of reducing them to practice. But in any event, they put their distinctive imprint on the matter.

None of this is as improbable as it might at first seem. If one takes into view only the parochial character of higher education in eighteenth-century America, the poverty of elementary education in those corners where it existed at all, and the preoccupation with day-to-day survival that marked the lives of all but a handful, then it is of course downright presumptuous to think of ranking the Americans with the likes of major British and French thinkers. And while it would be mean-spirited to begrudge Brissot de Warville his thrill on visiting the Harvard College library in 1788—"The heart of a Frenchman beats faster on finding Racine, Montesquieu, and the *Encyclopédie* in a place where one hundred and fifty years ago the savage still puffed his calumet"—one dare not infer too much from such tokens of cultivated taste and understanding.[2] Yet pause we must, for along with its unpropitious circumstances America presented another facet of its everyday life, equally germane but vastly more hopeful: the European population of mainland British America possessed an uncommonly high level of political literacy. By drawing on over a century and a half of experience and observation and on a powerfully present constitutional and legal heritage, the colonists had acquired a notable political education. Nor is that all. Their political education was made even more impressive by the constitutional struggle that culminated in the declaration of American independence and in the assertion of peoplehood and nationhood. It is especially in that context that one ought to turn our theme

2. J. P. Brissot de Warville, *Nouveau Voyage dans les États-Unis de l'Amérique Septentrionale, fait en 1788*, 3 vols. (Paris: Chez Buisson, 1791), 1:132.

about and ask, what is the place of the Enlightenment in America?

(( ))

Edmund Burke was not mistaken in viewing the Americans as a people still in the gristle. Their English heritage (or at least their interpretation of that heritage) had done much to help shape their hopes and fears. But having said that, and having made due allowance for the influence of biology, custom, geography, and sheer pigheadedness, we have still more to explain in trying to account for the Americans' behavior and cast of mind. This evolving people displayed, throughout their struggles with Whitehall and beyond, a broad range of beliefs and principles rightly associated with the Enlightenment.

The colonists certainly set great store by their charters and their charter rights, but it would be misleading to trace this concern to some infatuation with the mystery of wax and parchment. If anything, their prevailing taste and argument ran toward coolness and demystification. Long custom and prescriptive rights were cherished, not dismissed out of hand, but at least some of the colonists knew that one would pay dearly in turning a blind eye toward those unjust and absurd accretions that could and should otherwise be removed. Worshipful respect was no harmless pastime, and there was good reason to believe that those who most promoted such adulation stood most to gain by it. America, inching toward revolution and independence, was already a prefiguration of Missouri, a vast "Show Me State." Only by piercing the pleasing illusions of power could one expose to withering sunlight the worm within. The purging of the inevitable corruptions was a high civic duty.

Nor was this the only reason to demystify the processes of governance and render public what had hitherto been confined to closed quarters. Ultimately, the enjoyment of public liberty and private rights depended upon the existence of rationally defensible social arrangements. It would not do to presume trustworthiness in governors, because it may be the superior confidence man who most inspires confidence. "Jealousy" was the word that eighteenth-century Americans so frequently invoked: jealousy of political power, jealousy for one's rights. The desire to maintain one's guard and not let up being wary led the Americans to insist on holding government and governors to some rational standards.

Predictably, adherence to such standards might argue for simplification: streamlining institutions, sloughing off the now-odious excrescences of feudal modes and orders, clarifying chains of command, prescribing periodic accountability for budgets and policies, even such simple reforms as fixing salaries and posting fees for public services. A government posited on the public's right to know would be a government that could give a clear account of what it was up to— or at the least a government that could not successfully seek shelter in halls of mirrors or in labyrinths of its own devising.

But less predictably, rational standards might also argue for complication. At least in the American revolutionary context, the public good was commonly conflated with the end of rendering the enjoyment of private rights more secure. With this end in mind some were led to turn their thoughts to likely dangers. Reason, not to say experience, suggested that responsible government was not simply responsive government. Among the few unequivocal lessons to be drawn from history was this: that plebiscitary democracy had not proved a healthy environment for liberty. Thus, a government founded on rational principles would not mistake simplicity for safety or dismiss checks and balances as the last refuge of some self-serving faction. Rather, some fence or great barrier had to be erected, some means contrived that would be equal to whatever threatened to put the public good in jeopardy. Making that judgment would tax available statesmanship to its limits.

Demanding as that process might be, the standard for judgment was nonetheless clear and at hand. The Americans' touchstone would be utility. It would be futile to belabor this or document it at any length. Benjamin Franklin's *Autobiography* is one long paean to the beauties of utility, to clean streets and effective stoves, to convenient libraries and a ready fire department. Just as the thousands of illustrations in Diderot's and d'Alembert's *Encyclopédie* showed the beauty of rational means in the production and manufacture of items of everyday use, so too did Franklin's art drive that message home. Utility no longer would have to bear the onus of being the antonym of nobility; rather, the reverse. In a famous address to Europeans printed on his press at Passy, Franklin warned the prospective emigrant against going to America if he "has no other Quality to recommend him but his Birth. In Europe it has indeed its Value, but it is a Commodity that cannot be carried to a worse Market than to that of America. . . . If he has any useful Art, he is welcome; and if he exercises it and behaves well, he will be respected by all that know him; but a mere Man of Quality, who on that Account wants to live upon the Public, by some Office or Salary, will be despis'd and disregarded."[3]

Every claim to public regard and support thus would be compelled to answer for itself, What good was it?—meaning (more often than not), how would it help to make life more convenient, economical, and safe? This examination process was not to deny that there were other dimensions to life beyond such calculations but to insist that high-sounding claims and grand pretensions confront this insistently deflating query. In the past, indifference to such seemingly low considerations had led to a severe misallocation of scarce resources and to a haughtiness that could not conceal from sober republican scrutiny the incompetence and injustice of the mighty. In bringing high pretensions down to earth, so-

3. Franklin, "Information to Those Who Would Remove to America," Feb. 1784, in Benjamin Franklin, *Writings*, edited by J. A. Leo Lemay (New York: Library of America, 1987), 976–77.

ciety might bury the evil and harness the good. Such, at least, was the expectation.

This insistence upon public scrutiny, public accountability, and general utility rested on a revised understanding of popular consent. The necessity for public consent was of course no new discovery. Long before the Bourbons discarded the custom, the coronation ceremonies of the French had included an opportunity for the assembled people to cry out their assent to the monarch's elevation. But in an age when the franchise was rare and always narrowly confined at that, when representation was more often virtual than real, consent had rather to be inferred than observed. Further, what could it mean to speak of popular consent in a country believed to be peopled with inert nonentities? One thinks of Turgot's characterization of the French parish as a collection of huts not more passive than their tenants. Here was no fit matter for forming a public, and yet a public in the emphatic sense was most wanted.

The American revolutionaries acted on a different understanding of what their people were and might be, and their early efforts at state constitution-making gave formal expression to that insight. Popular consent was now seen not as something tacit and presumed (for want of public outcry to the contrary), but rather as an active voicing of the public mind. What is more, that act of consent was seen less as a spontaneous effusion of popular sentiment than as a deliberate response to a studied effort to win and deserve that assent. The formation, cultivation, and guidance of that public would pose the greatest challenge to the new, enlightened science of politics.

Here arises one of the most awkward features of the Enlightenment in America. Everyone knows that the Enlightenment was intended to be a mass enlightenment. Ultimately all people, even the most humble and insignificant, were to be disabused of the wicked fictions by means of which they had been manipulated and wronged. The thinkers who proclaimed this task were not of one mind on how this great project should be undertaken. Thomas Hobbes relied on a trickle-down theory, expecting large, good social consequences to follow from the adoption of his *Leviathan* as a required text in the universities. Through "Cato's Letters," John Trenchard and Thomas Gordon aimed at a broader audience, as did the editors and authors of the *Encyclopédie.* Finally, pamphleteering and electioneering were not beneath the dignity of those who under other circumstances might have contented themselves with more abstruse studies. Yet whatever the means of popular enlightenment, the instigators or engineers of that project were by no means run-of-the-mill types. Regardless of their social origins, they were distinguished from their fellows by abilities, energies, training, acuity, or dedication. The fomenters and conductors of the new, enlightened popular consent were an elite. What was to be their continuing relation to the many?

Some historians have maintained that many of the American revolutionary leaders expected that the deferential habits which allegedly were characteristic of colonial life would persist, and that these leaders (and not only the high Federalists among them) were surprised by the postrevolutionary turn in American political and social life. That theory is at least open to debate and discussion. For the public was being called in turn to resist the policies of King and Parliament, to support the Revolution, to persist in fighting the British to final victory, and to establish new state and federal governments; and if the contemporary characterizations of that public were more than empty flattery, then it was a public expected to take an active part in judging and shaping policy. True, the new American regime was no direct democracy, but neither was it designed for a people to be ruled by those who were their betters and were acknowledged by them to be their betters. Henceforth the people might be led, not ruled, and by leaders of their own choosing. Now the people were situated so as to be able to choose stupidly or well. Now they would be compelled to live with the consequences of their choices, having no one to blame other than themselves.

This characterization might seem too simple, too sanguine, even false to the spirit of the plainspoken American founders. Did not Jefferson acknowledge that "a choice by the people themselves is not generally distinguished for it's wisdom"?[4] And was not Madison, that cool proponent of a politics of reason, compelled to assert publicly that "the most rational government will not find it a superfluous advantage, to have the prejudices of the community on its side"?[5] Even more to the point is Madison's frank—if private—admission that the adoption of the proposed Constitution would turn less on its genuine merits than on "a general confidence of the people in those who may recommend it." There are, he reminded a wavering friend, "subjects to which the capacities of the bulk of mankind are unequal, and on which they must and will be governed by those with whom they happen to have acquaintance and confidence."[6] Yet having conceded this much as to the fragility of their cause, these American enlighteners were not prepared to give up their efforts to prove mankind capable of being their own governors. Instead, they insisted again and again that the people "must arm themselves with the power which knowledge gives." Accordingly, they promoted institutions and arrangements to "throw that light over the public mind which is the best security against crafty & dangerous encroachments on the public liberty." Failing that, a "popular Government, without popular information, or the means of acquiring it, is but a Prologue to a Farce or a Tragedy; or, perhaps both."[7]

4. Thomas Jefferson to Edmund Pendleton, 26 Aug. 1776, *The Papers of Thomas Jefferson*, edited by Julian P. Boyd et al., 25 vols. to date (Princeton: Princeton University Press, 1950–), 1:503.

5. Jacob E. Cooke, ed., *The Federalist* (Middletown, Conn.: Wesleyan University Press, 1961), no. 49, 340.

6. James Madison to Edmund Randolph, 10 Jan. 1788, *The Papers of James Madison*, edited by William T. Hutchinson et al., 10 vols. (Chicago: University of Chicago Press, 1962–77), 10:355–56.

7. James Madison to William T. Barry, 4 Aug. 1822, *The Writings*

Challenging as self-governance would be to the people at large, it placed in an even more delicate situation those natural *aristoi* of whom Jefferson and Adams spoke without embarrassment. Henceforward, those individuals whose rare qualities gave them singular abilities, opportunities, and duties would be obliged to maintain a low profile. At the very least they would have to advance themselves with discretion, for while the public demanded candor and openness, it would not brook anything smacking of condescension. Readers of Franklin's *Autobiography* would learn from its account of his secret society, the Junto, how to influence public opinion on particular occasions and prepare the minds of people for changes in public policy. The lesson was clear: popular leadership called the cues from the fourth row, not the stage.

In addressing these features of American revolutionary thought and relating them to that movement called the Enlightenment, I have seen fit to emphasize the public and political character of that thought. But this is only part of the story, for a major concern of the Americans' political program was to secure an enlarged private sphere. In that realm, placed as far as practicable beyond public control and even public scrutiny, men and women would be free to live their lives, pursuing happiness according to their lights. The consequences have been momentous—not only in America, where they have been writ large, but anywhere in the world where Enlightenment principles have been able to make themselves heard. I can only sketch some of these consequences in the most cursory way.

One change that was to strike Tocqueville with special force as he contemplated democratic mores was that which overtook the catalogue of the virtues. The quickest way to see this shift is to inspect the list that Benjamin Franklin offered in his scheme to achieve moral perfection, paying attention

---

of James Madison, edited by Gaillard Hunt, 9 vols. (New York: G. P. Putnam's Sons, 1900–1910), 9:103, 105.

to those virtues that are named and how they are defined, and to those that are silently dropped. Suffice it to say that Aristotle's great-souled man or Teresa of Avila or a dozen others whose lives might be culled from philosophy, literature, and devotional tracts pass from view. The models are more modest, the virtues almost within one's reach, the whole project of bettering oneself subject to a method that invites dogged determination rather than transcendent sacrifice. It is the promise of the exercise video and the health club in the moral sphere.

These are virtues that help me feel better about myself, physically as well as psychically. The utility of these social virtues is evident in the way they focus my energies on exactly those activities that are likely to make my life more comfortable. Since the body is no longer an object of revulsion—hair shirts and flagellation are out—and since I believe that my endless desire for decent comfort can be furthered, perhaps even gratified, with one or two more acquisitions, my thoughts run in that direction. I am now free to bend my efforts to the commerce that promises to deliver what is wanting. Moreover, I am developing the habits and traits that make my relations with others, especially strangers, go more smoothly. Just as the rules of Franklin's Junto were drawn with a view to keeping its members from disgusting each other, so the new moral code aims at raising somewhat the common level of decency in everyday life. Having attained that much, society should be less inclined to undertake grander but more meddlesome projects.

This taming or moderating effect is seen nowhere more clearly than in matters of religion. The human impulse to hasten others to their salvation, by words if possible, by the stake if need be, was one of the sorest points for the Enlighteners. Quite apart from the anticlericalism of some, the atheism of others, and the deism of still others, they were as one in deploring this temper of righteous harassment and persecution. Their principles and practices were directed at rendering the divine civil or (if that is too strong) at rendering claims resting on divine authority civil. To the extent that religious belief and practice could be treated as private, the genuine benefits of religious teaching would be enhanced and its capacity to foster hateful, even murderous, thoughts reduced. Though this private sphere frowned on martyrdom and did little to foster intense camaraderie, it did welcome good neighborliness.

Some find a society steeped in such thinking thin and vapid, like watery soup. Looking at this world we have inherited, these critics end up pining for the comforting closeness, shared enthusiasms, and dedication of a genuine community. Voting in school board elections and rooting for the hometown team are not enough. They scorn the petty materialism that crowds out other thoughts. They deplore the coolness of social life, the distance and distancing between fellows that individualism invites. They take this social attenuation to be one of the intended or unintended consequences of Enlightenment doctrine, and they fault the doctrine accordingly. More often than not, this latter-day Rousseauan yearning also silently presupposes a little world untainted by the severities of Genevan pastors or Parisian Montagnards. In wishing for genuine community, these critics do not expect to be noticeably cramped themselves.

If the Enlighteners, the objects of these criticisms, had illusions as well, they ran in different directions. Those reformers, both in America and in Europe, thought they had reasonable cause for hope and accordingly entertained great expectations. For their program as a whole promised a vast liberation of mankind from what was rotten, a restoration of what was sound, and a redirection of thoughts and energies toward what was sensible. By enlarging the sphere of individual choice even while raising people's estimates of themselves, they meant to honor the species. They thought they were only giving it its due. Our present-day inclination to conflate hopefulness with naiveté makes it hard for us to take a proper measure of these singular thinkers, even to see them singly and to assess each according to his merits. Just as

Jefferson was no Voltaire, so was Madison no Condorcet, and Franklin no Robespierre. That difference has something to do with what is distinctively American about the Enlightenment in America.

(( ))

The vast paper record left by those who participated in the American revolutionary struggle and in the establishment of new constitutional governments bears powerful witness to the presence and vitality of Enlightenment thought on these shores. From Northampton to Mecklenburg and Charleston, ordinary folk and fancy people spoke in accents that philosophers and English radical Whigs and Scottish social theorists could recognize and, by and large, approve. Yet the course of American revolutionary and constitutional development was its own. This revolution did not devour its own children (once the Loyalists were removed from the scene). Here failed constitutions were replaced without severing a single head. Whatever resentments and envy existed among the white colonists, they seem not to have left so permanent and prominent a mark as among the French.

Well, of course; America was not France. That was known before Louis Hartz, even before Alexis de Tocqueville. Thomas Jefferson, John Adams, John Jay all saw that with their own eyes and left records of their revulsion at much of what they observed abroad. For all their pretensions, the very rich among the Americans who chose to live high—the First Families of Virginia, Robert Morris, the Hudson River patroons—never amounted to a *noblesse*. To that extent, the fury that seethed among the French (and not only among those desperate for a crust of bread) had no proper object in America.

Nonetheless, the difference in how Enlightenment theory fared in the two places is striking. And it is not enough to say, "Well, the Americans were English," for so too were Paine and Priestley and Price. Rather, I think, the difference can be traced in large measure to the Americans' first-hand experience in self-government and the French thinkers' general lack thereof. Most of the Americans who gave voice to the premises of the revolution and shaped the new successor governments had actually served in legislatures. They learned from that work. Even Washington had served in the Virginia House of Burgesses, on top of learning the hard way by having to deal with state and confederal legislators while he commanded the army. Indeed, the collective experience of the Americans in the ways of popular government reached back to the early days of colonization. The several colonies had been, and as states continued to be, arenas of political experimentation. They learned or didn't learn different lessons, but in any case they developed habits that served as restraints on pure theorizing.

These habits led to what from one point of view was an appalling lack of theoretical clarity and coherence. A Turgot viewing early state constitution-making could deplore what he took to be the Americans' senseless aping of inappropriate and irrational British institutions. It struck him as incongruous that a rational people free to make a clean sweep of things should show so little faith in their own good sense. Yet from the standpoint of the American *philosophe* par excellence, Thomas Jefferson, the attractions of a blank slate were both real and delusive. The most clear and distinct language of a spanking new law would still have to be parsed and explicated. In shucking off the accretions of the ancient common law, one would only then be free—indeed obliged—to reinvent a new one. Here was a thankless task. Likewise, in crying up the cause of popular government, neither Jefferson nor his partner James Madison forgot the hard lessons each had learned while serving in the Virginia legislature and in the Continental Congress. They knew an elective despotism when they saw one, and they were intent on making a preemptive strike against it. They knew how the principle of representation might guard against the excesses of political enthusiasm—or exacerbate them. With a prudence born of practice and close observation, they had a deep sense of the dangers lurking not only in institutions but in human nature itself. These eloquent defenders and advocates of self-government were remarkably free from some common Enlightenment delusions, and in this they were not alone among the Americans.

In sum, the Enlightenment in America retained its hope and its promise: a private sphere for free consciences and free markets, a public sphere for securing the conditions for peace and general prosperity. Also preserved was the commitment to general enlightenment, from common township schools to John Quincy Adams's nursing of the Smithsonian Institution. None of this, however, could be produced magically from above. There could be no *lit de justice*, no *Six Edicts* of Turgot that would circumvent the political process and impose upon the selfish and recalcitrant the good they were mindlessly spurning. The Americans gambled on long, but not longer odds. By respecting the people's ability to choose, they took care to try to enable them to choose well. The political institutions and social arrangements that the American leaders proposed would, if adopted, be an extension of the people's education. If much was left unprovided for, if what they did provide dulled the taste for finer fare, that was not the last word. The Enlighteners in America always expected their successors to try to do better.

3

A Dialogue of Fathers and Sons

Just as the founders of the American republics looked back to a past that they both cherished and rejected, so too did they look forward to a future that might cherish and yet also in some sense reject them. Although the founders were believers in self-evident truths, in inalienable rights, in the lasting correctness of the principles of republican government, they were far from insisting on the fixity of each and every feature of their thought and work. Pleased though they were with much of what they had wrought, they had not exhausted their hopes. They began with the American people as they found them. They flattered themselves in thinking that, thanks to their constitutional regime, the American people would in time grow stronger, wealthier, and wiser—and to that extent freer. The founders neither expected nor desired the mindless adulation of their successors or the routine thoughtless application of their principles. Yes, they counted on the people's growing habituated to certain forms of thinking and acting, and even on their affectionate attachment to those familiar ways. Beyond those particular attachments, however, was to be a growing calm general understanding of what it takes to rule oneself. In looking forward to that, each succeeding generation would have something to labor for and to look up to.

Never far from the thoughts of a Washington, Franklin, Madison, Rush, Adams, or Jefferson was the concern for developing this kind of intelligent self-awareness in the people at large. Ultimately the success of the experiment would turn on that. Unless the people knew enough to be aware of their rights and cared enough to act in concert with others to secure those rights—in short, unless they were mindful of the demands and risks and opportunities of self-governance— the founders' brave experiment would falter or fail. The founders could neither give guarantees about the outcome nor refrain from pointing toward and working for a favored outcome. With high self-consciousness they bequeathed what they considered a goodly heritage, one that permitted their heirs to show what they could rise to. If the founders thought they could do no more, it is equally clear that they thought they could do no less.

The sons of the founders likewise had a double vision. The generations of John Quincy Adams and of Abraham Lincoln saw their fathers' legacy as entailing upon them great burdens and great hopes. Although the American war of independence might be over, the task of founding was not yet complete. For both fathers and sons the establishment of revolutionary constitutionalism in America marked not only a culmination of an age-old struggle but a promising and demanding new beginning. Beyond the peaceful enjoyment of rights, beyond the anticipated domestic prosperity and tranquillity, lay the challenge of using those goods to achieve something even finer. It was to that promise that some of the leading figures of the early generations turned their thoughts, propelled by a fervent belief in the power of education broadly conceived. Retracing those thoughts may help us to see more clearly the kind of regime they envisioned.

(( ))

Speaking in general terms of the founders' stance toward their past tempts us into simplifications, even oversimplifications. In fact, the founders' attitudes were neither simple nor undiscriminating. Along with their great "nay" to leading features of the old established order went a deep regard for their English inheritance of constitutional rights, traditional liberties, and the rule of law. While they were confident that earlier theory or political science might now be surpassed, they believed no less that the lessons of the past, historical experience, remained the best if not the only guide.

Yet in the new world aborning, it was the America of their design and not some mythic past that would be the model. America's proclaimed and freely chosen goals would be a cautionary reminder to itself and might serve as an inspiration to others. Thus one might say with Alexander Hamilton that "it remains for us to justify the revolution by its fruits."[1] Although this recurring theme was invoked in efforts to move a reluctant public opinion, it was more than a rhetorical trope. The founders thought that their own good names were at stake in the success or failure of the American experiment; or rather, they staked their fame on the larger meaning of that experiment—the still unresolved question of a people's capacity to govern itself well. While the goal no longer was cast as the Puritans' holy city upon a hill, the new Zion, it remained in the founders' eyes an eminence intensely interesting to mankind at large.[2] In making large claims and

1. Hamilton, "Second Letter from Phocion," Apr. 1784, *The Papers of Alexander Hamilton*, edited by Harold C. Syrett et al., 27 vols. (New York: Columbia University Press, 1961–87), 3:557.

2. See James Madison, "Address to the States, by the United States

asserting high hopes for their new regime, the founders were in a way seeking to correct for the kind of public political life likely to flourish there. Such aspirations could call to mind the larger meaning and value of the experiment, a prod especially needful in times of great heat over small issues. Where so much of ordinary life narrowed the citizenry's thoughts and tugged them earthward, reminders of high principle, grand example, and broad significance would be indispensable. In this sense the American heritage might save the Americans from themselves.

Securing that high ground, and erecting upon it something truly worth looking up to, would require a peculiar education—one fitted for this people, in this place, and in these circumstances.[3] The most pressing task was to persuade that people of their need for such an education. It was likely that men and women so preoccupied with the urgencies of making a living or of improving their economic situation would be little inclined to adorn or refine whatever they already judged serviceable enough. Indeed, at this distance it is hard for us to say how much of the perceived popular resistance to grander projects stemmed from external necessities or ignorant self-satisfaction.

Thus Benjamin Rush, for example, in thinking about the kind of education suitable for America, had no difficulty accepting the usual priorities of life in an undeveloped country: "Our principal business should be to explore and apply its resources, all of which press us to enterprize and haste.

---

in Congress Assembled," 26 Apr. 1783, *The Papers of James Madison*, edited by William T. Hutchinson et al., 10 vols. (Chicago: University of Chicago Press, 1962–77), 6:493–94. For Alexander Hamilton's formulation, see Jacob E. Cooke, ed., *The Federalist* (Middletown, Conn.: Wesleyan University Press, 1961), no. 1, 3.

3. See the discerning and detailed analysis in Lorraine Smith Pangle and Thomas L. Pangle, *The Learning of Liberty: The Educational Ideas of the American Founders* (Lawrence: University Press of Kansas, 1993).

Under these circumstances, to spend four or five years in learning two dead languages [Greek and Latin], is to turn our backs upon a gold mine, in order to amuse ourselves in catching butterflies."[4] But Rush did not view himself as the founding father of George F. Babbitt's Zenith. From the outset of the struggle for independence, he was intent on getting Americans to distinguish the short-range measures that proclaimed a revolution from the long-range measures that secured a revolution. Quite apart from his private distaste for those who "have little relish for the 'feast of reason and the flow of soul,'" Rush had sufficient political incentives to work for an America that was more than all business. Nothing short of the reconstitution of the manners of the people would secure them against monarchical temptations and aristocratic subversion. "Republican seminaries" would go far in inculcating the technical skills and moral lessons that might render the people safe and knowing guardians of their own liberty.[5]

That same great objective lies at the core of the far-reaching reforms Jefferson proposed for Virginia in the early years of the revolution. While some of those reforms were manifestly changes in institutions—in the way property was passed on from one generation to the next, in the way religious organizations were supported, in the way local civil

4. Benjamin Rush, "Observations upon the Study of the Latin and Greek Languages," in *Essays, Literary, Moral and Philosophical*, 2d ed. (Philadelphia, 1806), 39.

5. Benjamin Rush, "Address to the People of the United States" (1787), in *Principles and Acts of the Revolution*, compiled by Hezekiah Niles, "centennial offering" (New York: A. S. Barnes & Co., 1876), 234; Rush to Arthur Lee, 4 May 1774, *Letters of Benjamin Rush*, edited by Lyman H. Butterfield, Memoirs of the American Philosophical Society, vol. 30, pts. 1 and 2 (Princeton: Princeton University Press for the American Philosophical Society, 1951), 1:85; Rush, "Of the Mode of Education Proper in a Republic" (1786), *The Selected Writings of Benjamin Rush*, edited by Dagobert D. Runes (New York: Philosophical Library, 1947), 94.

government conceived of its functions—institutional change was only part of the story. Viewed as a whole, Jefferson's revisal of Virginia's laws may be thought of as an elaborate exercise in popular political education.[6] It is quite obvious that Jefferson wished to see that all the free boys and girls of the commonwealth learned the three R's and the useful lessons of history and, likewise, that those students of "the best learning and most hopeful genius and disposition" should be able to attend (at the public's expense) a college properly reconstituted to reflect and help secure "the late change in the form of our government."[7] He did not, however, leave it at that. Taking great pains and descending to the smallest particulars, Jefferson also constructed an elaborate network of responsibilities and accountabilities that involved not only overseers and aldermen but teachers, electors, and even students. This network would offer more than a lesson in booklearning for the young, for Jefferson was intent on explaining by example precisely what he understood by self-governance. Here were lessons in living republicanism to be learned and applied at all levels by the citizenry. To this end he contrived institutions that would bring individuals together linked in common cause. Their mutual involvements would make it necessary for them to develop skills of listening and speaking, of thinking and judging—in short, of behaving like a people who deserved a free society and would be capable of sustaining it. Nothing less could secure the revolution's promise.

Although the contents and emphases of their several educational projects differed, both Benjamin Rush and Thomas Jefferson agreed with Noah Webster in this: a proper system of education would fit every citizen to choose others and be

6. This theme is developed in Ralph Lerner, *The Thinking Revolutionary: Principle and Practice in the New Republic* (Ithaca, N.Y.: Cornell University Press, 1987), 60–90.

7. Revisal of the Laws, Bill nos. 79–80, *The Papers of Thomas Jefferson*, edited by Julian P. Boyd et al., 25 vols. to date (Princeton: Princeton University Press, 1950–), 2:533, 538.

chosen in turn for places of public trust.[8] For Rush, the moral teachings of the Bible and the pacific calculations of commerce would point young republicans in the right direction. For Jefferson, the stirring yet unhappy histories of earlier republics would yield useful lessons for moderns eager to avoid the past's fatal political errors. For Webster, a distinctive speller, reader, and dictionary would be the vehicles for shaping a new American nationality. None of these founders was willing to leave the desired outcomes to the workings of chance; there was simply too much at stake.

Looking beyond schooling, James Wilson voiced the expectation that political participation itself might become a most valuable means of education, drawing individuals out of their workaday concerns and accustoming them to the ways of dignified citizenship.

> The man who enjoys the right of suffrage, on the extensive scale which is marked by our constitutions, will naturally turn his thoughts to the contemplation of publick men and publick measures. The inquiries he will make, the information he will receive, and his own reflections on both, will afford a beneficial and amusing employment to his mind. I am far from insinuating, that every citizen should be an enthusiast in politicks, or that the interests of himself, his family, and those who depend on him for their comfortable situation in life, should be absorbed in Quixote speculations about the management or the reformation of the state. But there is surely a golden mean in things; and there can be no real incompatibility between the discharge of one's publick, and that of his private duty. Let private industry receive the warmest encouragement;

8. Thomas Jefferson, *Notes on the State of Virginia*, edited by William Peden (Chapel Hill: University of North Carolina Press for the Institute of Early American History and Culture, 1954), 146–49; Noah Webster, "On the Education of Youth in America" (1788), in *A Collection of Essays and Fugitiv Writings on Moral, Historical, Political and Literary Subjects* (Boston, 1790), 23–26.

for it is the basis of publick happiness. But must the bow of honest industry be always bent? At no moment shall a little relaxation be allowed? . . .

Under our constitutions, a number of important appointments must be made at every election. To make them is, indeed, the business only of a day. But it ought to be the business of much more than a day, to be prepared for making them well. When a citizen elects to office—let me repeat it—he performs an act of the first political consequence. He should be employed, on every convenient occasion, in making researches after proper persons for filling the different departments of power; in discussing, with his neighbours and fellow citizens, the qualities, which ought to be possessed by those, who enjoy places of publick trust; and in acquiring information, with the spirit of manly candour, concerning the manners and characters of those, who are likely to be candidates for the publick choice.

A habit of conversing and reflecting on these subjects, and of governing his actions by the result of his deliberations, would produce, in the mind of the citizen, a uniform, a strong, and a lively sensibility to the interests of his country.[9]

For all their preoccupations with the urgencies of the hour, the most notable founders never lost sight of the needs of the morrow. Thus an anxious John Adams, even while spurning the seductive pleasures of French royal gardens and palaces in the name of his pressing public duties, still could sharply distinguish what was expected of him from what he expected of his descendants. "I must study Politicks and War that my sons may have liberty to study Mathematicks and Philosophy. My sons ought to study Mathematicks and Phi-

9. James Wilson, *Lectures on Law*, in *The Works of James Wilson*, edited by Robert Green McCloskey, 2 vols. (Cambridge: Belknap Press of Harvard University Press, 1967), 1:404–5.

losophy, Geography, natural History, Naval Architecture, navigation, Commerce and Agriculture, in order to give their Children a right to study Painting, Poetry, Musick, Architecture, Statuary, Tapestry and Porcelaine."[10] Establishing America's separate and equal station among the powers of the earth—politically, militarily, and commercially—was the first order of business, not the last.

A paterfamilias plans for his offspring, a founding father plans for his country: whatever the resemblances, the difficulties are incommensurable. Postrevolutionary youth had so much to learn, an old Jefferson complained to his older comrade Adams; yet the young were not of a mind to learn from anyone. One would hope that experience might dent their mistaken self-sufficiency and that in time they might come to value education on a broad scale. Meanwhile, however, Jefferson's thoughts ran toward supplying the lack that young America could not yet detect: a university whose structure, curriculum, and faculty would be designed for this new kind of society.[11]

His partner in founding the new University of Virginia thought likewise. James Madison's long and thwarted efforts on behalf of public education had left him well qualified to respond when a hopeful official of a young state sought counsel from a weary veteran of an old. True, Virginia had little enough to point to with pride in this respect, but Madison could anticipate and answer all the shortsighted

10. John Adams to Abigail Adams, post–12 May 1780, *Adams Family Correspondence*, edited by L. H. Butterfield et al., 4 vols. (Cambridge: Belknap Press of Harvard University Press, 1963–73), 3:342. This development took one generation longer than John Adams had calculated: John, John Quincy, Charles Francis, Henry.

11. Thomas Jefferson to John Adams, 5 July 1814, *The Adams-Jefferson Letters: The Complete Correspondence between Thomas Jefferson and Abigail and John Adams*, edited by Lester J. Cappon, 2 vols. (Chapel Hill: University of North Carolina Press for the Institute of Early American History and Culture, 1959), 2:434.

arguments that neighboring Kentuckians might adduce against a proposed general system of state-funded education. He had a ready answer to objections prompted by democratic indifference, fear of elitism, and parsimony. But most revealing, perhaps, were Madison's political appeals to a free people, appeals that sought to transcend real or alleged social divisions: "[I]t is certain that every Class is interested in establishments which give to the human mind its highest improvements, and to every Country its truest and most durable celebrity." It could be assumed that the quality of public lawmaking and of public life would all be enhanced by the diffused effects of "Learned Institutions." Beyond that, however, lay this even larger inducement:

> Throughout the Civilized World, nations are courting the praise of fostering Science and the useful Arts, and are opening their eyes to the principles and the blessings of Representative Government. The American people owe it to themselves, and to the cause of free Government, to prove by their establishments for the advancement and diffusion of Knowledge, that their political Institutions, which are attracting observation from every quarter, and are respected as Models, by the new-born States in our own Hemisphere, are as favorable to the intellectual and moral improvement of Man as they are conformable to his individual & social Rights. What spectacle can be more edifying or more seasonable, than that of Liberty & Learning, each leaning on the other for their mutual and surest support?[12]

The promise of revolutionary constitutionalism had still to be fulfilled.

12. James Madison to William T. Barry, 4 Aug. 1822, *The Writings of James Madison*, edited by Gaillard Hunt, 9 vols. (New York: G. P. Putnam's Sons, 1900–1910), 9:104–5, 107–8.

(( ))

That promise remained a challenge to the succeeding generation. To see this clearly one ought first to address the same questions to the sons: What was their stance toward *their* past? What did they see as their most pressing needs? What did they take to be the longer-range needs of American society? In choosing John Quincy Adams and Abraham Lincoln as examples, one can hardly claim to have invoked representative types of the middle period of American history. But by the same token, one could hardly find individuals who had delved more profoundly into the questions at hand.

It is tempting to regard John Quincy Adams as a kind of resident alien in the nineteenth century. By temperament, training, and taste he belonged to his father's era. Yet it is also fair to say that John Quincy did not let his admiration for the revolution, and for those who made it, dull his critical faculties. The nineteenth century was barely six weeks old when, looking back, he heaped his scorn upon "the flood of philosophy which poured upon that self-conceited dupe, the eighteenth century."[13] A defensible belief in progress had overreached itself, with terrifying results. Believer though he was, John Quincy was not about to be carried away.

Lincoln was equally capable of distancing himself from "those old-time men" of '76 whose sentiments he confessed to loving so much; his stance was at least as complex as Adams's. On the one hand, he steadfastly presented himself as a conservative defender of the old policy of the fathers, especially when fending off attacks by adherents of Stephen A. Douglas who were portraying Lincoln as a revolutionary and a dis-

13. John Quincy Adams to Thomas Boylston Adams, 14 Feb. 1801, in *The Selected Writings of John and John Quincy Adams*, edited by Adrienne Koch and William Peden (New York: Alfred A. Knopf, 1946), 258.

rupter of union (*SW* 1:329, 2:120–22; *CW* 2:267, 3:535–38).[14] On the other hand, he presented himself as a modern, a believer in progress, one who took special delight in "the discovery of anything which is at once *new* and *valuable*" (*SW* 2:119, 99, 101; *CW* 3:534–35, 480, 482). He understood—and showed—the ease with which the founders' high ambitions could be dissected and demystified. But with equal ease Lincoln lampooned the snippy self-satisfaction and self-delusion of Douglas's "Young America" (*SW* 1:33–34, 89, 2:3–4, 7; *CW* 1:113, 278, 3:356–58, 360).

The proper bearing of sons toward fathers had to be at once modest and discriminating. If one approached the problem by first considering America's role in the world, the matter would appear in a clearer light. Lincoln's audience was all too ready to presume American superiority in inventiveness and to extrapolate from that to American superiority in general. In comparison, the rest of the world was immured in custom and ignorance (and increasingly so, it seemed, as one moved eastward). "In anciently inhabited countries, the dust of ages—a real downright old-fogyism—seems to settle upon, and smother the intellects and energies of man." It was in this context that Lincoln spoke of a new country as "most favorable—almost necessary—to the immancipation of thought, and the consequent advancement of civilization and the arts."

But this presumption in favor of the New World and of Young America (nothing of course is newer than "the most

14. The volume and page locations of all quotations from Lincoln are cited parenthetically in the text. References are to two editions, separated by a semicolon. The first reference is to Abraham Lincoln, *Speeches and Writings*, edited by Don E. Fehrenbacher, 2 vols. (New York: Library of America, 1989); the title is abbreviated *SW*. The second is to *The Collected Works of Abraham Lincoln*, edited by Roy P. Basler et al., 9 vols. (New Brunswick, N.J.: Rutgers University Press, 1953–55); the title is abbreviated *CW*. This theme is examined in detail in chapter 6.

current youth of the age") grievously underestimated the debt of the young to the old. We moderns "owe everything which distinguishes us from savages" to the legacy of Old Fogy—the habit of observation and reflection, the sundry discoveries and inventions that resulted from that habit, and finally, the gradual awareness that ordinary folk, too, are capable of rising to equality. "It is difficult for us, *now* and *here*, to conceive how strong this slavery of the mind was; and how long it did, of necessity, take, to break it's shackles, and to get a habit of freedom of thought, established." Analogously, Young America owed almost everything to the Old Fogy founders who had invented the country on a new principle, a principle that now appeared as old. Just as the one emancipation—that of the mind from a "false and under estimate of itself"—was the work not of a day but of a century, so too might be the other sort of emancipation. Here was a lesson that the followers of both Stephen A. Douglas and William Lloyd Garrison might take to heart (*SW* 2:3–10; *CW* 3:356, 358–63). There was a past to remember and cherish even as there was a past to overcome.

Indeed, it was the denigration of that older principle (Jefferson's "abstract truth, applicable to all men and all times"), and the consequent perversion of liberty to imperialistic purposes, that so exercised both Lincoln and John Quincy Adams. However, the open or covert sapping of those founding principles called not for their public repudiation and consignment to the rubbish heap of history but for a restoration or recovery of the "axioms of free society." No task was more urgent. Hence Lincoln (echoing the founders) could view popular education in the principles of the regime as "the most important subject which we as a people can be engaged in." Perhaps nothing less would suffice: an entire people had to become passionately attached to a system of rational liberty (*SW* 2:19, 1:4, 32–33, 36; *CW* 3:375–76, 1:8, 112, 115). Precisely because Abraham Lincoln and John Quincy Adams—like Henry Clay—saw an intimate connection between "the light of reason, and the love of liberty," they tended to view whatever jeopardized the one as likely to jeopardize the other (*SW* 1:270–71; *CW* 2:131).[15]

Neither Lincoln nor Adams found it easy to think of America's longer-range needs and opportunities abstracted from the festering wound of slavery. Perhaps this is only another way of saying that for both men "this is a world of compensations; and he who would *be* no slave, must consent to *have* no slave"; those whose private interest or ambition or passion made them indifferent or neutral toward the fundamental principle of human equality could not be trusted either to guard that principle or to respect it (*SW* 2:19; *CW* 3:376).[16] Just as the plainest print could not be read through a gold eagle, so too would an attitude of "don't care" obscure the foundations of the regime. The result would be a population coolly prepared to expand or contract human slavery depending on the comparative returns of alternative forms of investment, a population unilaterally disarmed of any principle by which it might combat the machinations of ruthless demagoguery. To contain or ward off those evils, John Quincy Adams and Lincoln sought to create a vast continental empire of liberty. Their commitments to internal improvements, free soil, free labor, indeed to an *educated* population of laborers, may be seen as so many ways of binding a diverse public in a diverse land to a singular and ennobling ideal.

15. See also John Quincy Adams to Richard C. Anderson, 27 May 1823, in *Selected Writings*, 345–52. None of this precluded the surprising turn of an impoverished European republicanism which showed "that the *arts* and *sciences* themselves, that genius, talents, and learning, are in the most enlightened periods of the human history liable to become objects of proscription to political fanaticism" (John Quincy Adams to John Adams, 27 July 1795, *Selected Writings*, 247).

16. See also Lincoln, *SW* 1:34–35, 402–3, and *CW* 1:114, 2:409–10, and John Quincy Adams, diary entry for 24 Nov. 1843, in *Selected Writings*, 407.

For both men there was a deep and continuing connection between the principles of American revolutionary constitutionalism and the moral and intellectual improvement of the human race. Accordingly, the project of reducing American principles to practice took on for them the hues of genuine nobility. For Lincoln this mighty effort was not simply an American achievement but an emphatically human one—the triumph of a particular people in a particular land to be sure, but with universal consequences (*SW* 2:101; *CW* 3:482).[17] To John Quincy Adams, speaking in an age when "the spirit of improvement [was] abroad upon the earth," it seemed inconceivable that a government charged with the powers enumerated in the Constitution should hold itself incapable of advancing the mechanical and elegant arts, literature, and "the sciences, ornamental and profound." Equally, it seemed to Adams churlish and "unworthy of a great and generous nation" not to join with other civilized nations in the exploration of the earth and the heavens. European contributions to those branches of science posed a direct challenge to the Americans—and to the grandest implications of their revolutionary principles. "But what, in the meantime, have *we* been doing?"[18] A people posing such a question to themselves could not be charged with holding only petty aspirations.

( )

Facing up to the founding has entailed for founders and successors alike a willingness to step back and take stock, to orient oneself toward the larger purposes that from the outset

17. See also the image of man as a miner who discovers and exploits the untapped treasures that constitute "the whole world, material, moral, and intellectual" (Lincoln, *SW* 2:5; *CW* 3:358).

18. John Quincy Adams, First Annual Message, 6 Dec. 1825, in *Selected Writings*, 360–64, 366–67; oration delivered before the Cincinnati Astronomical Society, 10 Nov. 1843, *Selected Writings*, 400–401, 405–6.

gave the revolutionary cause its impulse and meaning. In illustrating through word and deed their ways of respecting and transcending *their* past, those early fathers and sons have shown their successors in turn how to face up to their achievements. One cannot review the thoughts of those early revolutionary constitutionalists without being impressed by both their sobriety and hopefulness. If they cherished certain features of their colonial or imperial legacy, it was with a view to surpassing those older ways. If they expected this continent to serve as a testing ground for the conversion of their theoretical principles into homegrown practices, it was with more than half a thought to displaying models that others might be tempted to emulate and adapt. Treading a narrow path (and not always successfully) between pretension and parochialism, between bombast and pettiness, those fathers and sons acted on a common assumption. Here, they thought, was something that Americans of all kinds and conditions might most reasonably take pride in: a general willingness to face up to their own highest expectations. For founders and successors alike, the promise of America would always lie just over the horizon.

II

Re-visioning "Our Revolution"

4

What Manner of Speech?

Popular historians, intent on gratifying our desire to define and characterize whole eras, have responded in kind. With a few bold, simple strokes, they offer for our consideration pictures of an Age of Faith, an Age of Reason, an Industrial Age, and the like. Whatever bewilderment or sense of wonder may first have troubled our view of the past and prompted us to seek their help is in a sense quieted, at least for a while. Yet our satisfaction, such as it is, carries its own price. If we are to remain content with the likely tale they offer us, we have to suspend our native sense that in real life matters are not that simple and unambiguous. Indeed, if the historian's proffered certitude is to overcome our healthy misgiving or doubt, he or she must from first to last continue to persuade. The same might be said of any nontrivial use of history: lacking a demonstrative argument, the interpreter must find some way of making a probable case to an audience that may well be otherwise-minded, suspicious, indifferent, or easily bored.

These difficulties, formidable enough as they stand, are compounded further in the instances to be discussed in the following chapters. There, attention is to be focused not on historians "doing history," still less on philosophers thinking about "History," but on singular practical men of political affairs who make use of historical example and interpretation to advance their own policies and promote their own approaches toward the issues of their day. Recourse to the history of their respective national revolutions bespeaks, in these cases, neither mindless ritual nor antiquarianism. It testifies, rather, to considered judgments that *this* would be the fitting and effective way of reaching and shaping their public's mind.

Our readiness to dismiss such political uses of history as merely manipulative or (in the familiar pejorative sense of the term) rhetorical grows out of a currently strong predisposition to contextualize all statements. According to this school of thought, the surer truth behind any marshaling of reasons is that all such arguments need to be deeply discounted. Once we recognize how pervasively influential are social setting, habits of language, and other historical and cultural factors on our modes of thinking and arguing, any assertions of timeless truthfulness will stand stripped of their pretension and credibility. At most we may say that such claims are used to make the naive believe and the unruly behave—but with a view to someone else's present advantage.

This way of reading, I shall argue, is both reductive and overly simple. Although the immediate concern of these political men's efforts is a decision to be made today—a vote to do this or that, a practical expression of support or opposition—they most emphatically also have larger ends in view. Ultimately their longer focus is on the state of mind that is the substrate, as it were, of all such transient, particular decisions. Within that substrate, passionate attachments (and aversions) and reasoned argument work upon one another. When resorting to history—"our history"—to help make their case, these men must thus appeal to both the affective and rational parts of their public's souls. Not content merely to gain votes (although of course never for a moment losing sight of that objective), these politicians know they must also gain their countrymen's ears so as to gain their minds. For if they fail to bring that public into *their* peculiar ways of seeing and thinking, any seeming success on a narrow field of action will be but ephemeral.

The problem is how to secure an opening for reasoned discourse and reflection on the long term in a place where arguments don't always join, minds don't often meet, and premiums are paid for the short term. Few would mistake the hustings for a seminar room, the general public for a conventicle of philosophers. A politician, satisfied in his own mind of the justice and rationality of his cause, seeks out arguments that might bring others closer to his position, arguments that may rest on premises that are generally accepted rather than simply true. In acting and speaking thus, the politician behaves as might any advocate; and since the difficulties facing any would-be persuader of a citizenry have been a theme of Western reflection since at least the days of Socrates, there would seem to be little call for an intensive new investigation. Yet for all that, there are some politicians whose sustained efforts to reach their public are both exemplary and of lasting interest. Their uncommon use of common tools sets them apart. We are not apt to conflate the spirited arguments of Edmund Burke, Abraham Lincoln, and Alexis de Tocqueville with the subliminal manipulations of merchandisers of cosmetics, clothing, and cars. I shall try to make evident that politicians of their rank have in view not only a persuaded audience but a more thoughtful public. Especially singular and noteworthy is the manner in which they undertake to make their public rise in some sense above itself. For this alone they would deserve our renewed attention.

(( ))

If past is indeed prologue, the politician with a long view and a good voice will remind a people of their history. On hearing such a retelling by a gifted orator, a people may be moved either to be true to their past or to rid themselves of it. In either event the statesman's intention is both practical and philosophical. Drawing on collective memory, he remolds it. Ostentatiously disclaiming novelty or originality, he veils his art. In rehearsing the old story, he furthers his own new, or his people's renewed, political program.

Today's political science seems not to recognize this kind of activity. At least none of the usual tags—political rhetoric, propaganda, civil religion, the engineering of consent, political socialization—conveys the range, depth of analysis, and feeling that a master of this art of speaking can draw upon and evoke in an audience. Working at a level more fundamental than particular policies or the laws themselves, even while seeking to affect such policies and laws, the statesman aims to fix or reform the people's predispositions. These, when settled, make certain outcomes possible and others quite out of the question.

Today we have lost sight of the necessity that once led statesmen to concern themselves with these predispositions. We measure our officials by their readiness to do our bidding; we seek rather to be represented than ruled by those we call "public servants." And our political science follows suit. Plato, in contrast, viewed this persuasive art by which the people's fundamental orientations may be secured to be so much a part of politics that he integrated it into his code of law, which he set forth in the *Laws*, in the form of preludes or *prooimia* to the laws. Despite our contemporary oblivion about the need for such an art, there are within our own modern tradition those who do realize this need. In the most widely recognized instance, Thomas Jefferson manifested his awareness of it in his drafting of the Declaration of Independence and in some of his most celebrated proposed enactments to free the human mind.[1] My case studies here—Burke, Lincoln, and Tocqueville—remind us of how recently this art was in full flower, yet in order to find a term that adequately characterizes what these moderns are about, we may need to return to ancient political philosophy and to the medieval political science that built on it. Plato may have been the founder of this art, but, surprising though it may seem, Abū Naṣr al-Fārābī, a medieval student of Plato, was the first to make this art itself a topic of scientific analysis. This art was familiar within his own tradition as "dialectical theology" or *kalām*.[2]

It is helpful, I would submit, to consider some of these modern men's productions as indeed being forms of a political *kalām*. In distinguishing this Islamic religious science from both political science proper and jurisprudence, Fārābī defines it as an art enabling one "to argue in the defense of the specific opinions and actions stated explicitly by the founder of the religion, and against everything that opposes these opinions and actions."[3] Its stance, then, is defensive and protective; its point of reference some original intent. That which it would oppose or check is presented as being at odds

1. See the discussion of these bills in Ralph Lerner, *The Thinking Revolutionary: Principle and Practice in the New Republic* (Ithaca, N.Y.: Cornell University Press, 1987), 78–88.

2. For a synoptic overview see Muhsin Mahdi, "Philosophy and Political Thought: Reflections and Comparisons," *Arabic Sciences and Philosophy* 1 (1991): 9–29. The most recent comprehensive account of Fārābī's works (along with a bibliography of texts, translations, and interpretations) is Miriam Galston, *Politics and Excellence: The Political Philosophy of Alfarabi* (Princeton: Princeton University Press, 1990).

3. *The Enumeration of the Sciences* (*Iḥṣā' al-ʿUlūm*), chap. 5. An English translation is in *Medieval Political Philosophy: A Sourcebook*, edited by Ralph Lerner and Muhsin Mahdi (New York: Free Press of Glencoe, 1963), 27.

with, or subversive of, that earlier understanding. The threat
to the old may come as readily from those who expect too
much reason in politics as from those who behave as though
they expect too little. In neither case, however, can there be
any recovery of that earlier, purportedly sounder arrangement without recollection.

In urging his people to face up to their founding, the
speaker may well use locutions more typical of a family
member than of an archeologist or analytic philosopher. The
investigation the audience is urged to undertake (along with
the speaker, as it were) may be more or less probing but will
not seem philosophical and will surely not be distanced or
academic. For the intention, to repeat, is defensive; the argument oppositional, dialectical; the object under investigation
one's own. Still, for all its apologetic character, the arguments
of *kalām* are indeed arguments and thus may provide "a
place for reflexion and meditation, and hence for reason, in
the elucidation and defence of the content of the faith."[4] Nor
ought its defensive character to be taken as simply precluding
an innovative intent. "Necessity" may dictate change—
change that might even come close to touching fundamen-
tals—but wise legislators hardly need to be cautioned about
appearing unseemly. Their response to necessity will likely be
to present their own reformation as a correction of some
intervening distortion or corruption and certainly not as a
case of their overruling the founding legislator. Indeed, regardless of the reach of their corrections, the successors'
speech is less of reformation than of restoration.[5]

4. Louis Gardet, "'Ilm al-Kalām," in *The Encyclopaedia of Islam*,
new ed., vol. 3 (Leiden: E. J. Brill, 1971), 1142.

5. See Fārābī's "Summary of Plato's *Laws*" (*Talkhīṣ Nawāmīs
Aflāṭun*), discourse 7, sect. 11. The text is in *Alfarabius Compendium
Legum Platonis*, edited by Francesco Gabrieli (London: Warburg
Institute, 1952), 35.19–36.2 (Arabic), 27 (Latin).

(( ))

To speak in a modern Western context of a politician's dialectical theology is to invite disbelief, derision. It smacks of a world of imams, of fundamentalist polemics and God-intoxicated zealotry far removed from the electoral politics of government and loyal opposition. Furthermore, the examples I mean to adduce in the following pages are, to say the least, unusual candidates. Not only are they moderns; they are moderns each of whose political thinking presupposes a modern revolution made (to different degrees) on modern principles. Those principles in turn were presented by their philosophic progenitors to the world at large as rational, as carrying a force clear to even the meanest capacity. Here was a way of thinking that seemed to have as little need for rhetoric as for priestcraft. It is all the more striking, then, that these thoughtful men of practical affairs, heirs to that revolution in thought and deed, found it useful, even necessary, to appeal to history when addressing their public. If this bespeaks some earlier oversight or inadequacy in the modern rationalist project, it also bespeaks another reason for looking once again to earlier thinking about politics.

Yet it is also likely that those tenth-century Muslims who were Fārābī's contemporaries and immediate addressees were equally (although differently) caught off balance by his analysis. Certain features of his presentation in the *Enumeration of the Sciences* have the effect of making the familiar—in this case the traditional Islamic sciences of jurisprudence and dialectical theology—seem distant and abstract. Fārābī speaks of religions, not of Islam; and his point of departure is an analysis of the scope and methods of political science, not of the Koran. There is not even a nod acknowledging the massive presence of the divinely revealed Law, the *sharīʿa*, which constitutes the community and prescribes its definitive actions and opinions. Abstracting from the manifest differences among religions, Fārābī chooses to address the function of jurisprudence in "every religion" and to classify theologians according to the methods they adopt in defending "religions." He singles out as one of the special targets of dialectical theologians the kind of individual "who has reached the limit of human perfection," one "who is perfect in humanity." At the very least, this delicate reference shows the traditional Islamic sciences to stand in a certain tension with a political science whose basic questions and orientation are neither derived from nor dependent upon the revealed, supreme Law of the land.

The relationship between political science, jurisprudence, and *kalām* that is suggested by Fārābī's account is recognizable in our times and terms as well. Now as then, lawyers and judges are expected to keep within the framework of the regnant law. Its premises and prescriptions are their givens, and they take care to present their arguments and judgments as inferences and deductions drawn from the letter and intention of the lawgiver, be that the constitution or ordinary statutes. Nor are we today without our corresponding political *kalām*, often one falling neatly within Fārābī's typology of modes in which a community's way of life may be defended. Thus there is the defense that disclaims any merely rational justification, holding instead that there is a wisdom in our present arrangement—a product of, say, History—that surpasses any possible merely human contrivance. Similarly, there is the effort to harmonize earlier texts with current opinions to the maximum extent possible. With sufficient interpretive latitude, even inconvenient facts may be made to fit. Less lovely still are those attempts to return fire with more of the same: ad hominem arguments of many kinds, not excluding the use of shame, fear, and systematic "disinformation." It is safe to say that the arsenal of devices described by Fārābī has not diminished over time.

While these forms of political *kalām* are notorious in efforts to deal with external enemies (leading to censorship and the jamming of unwelcome electronic communications, for example), they are by no means limited to that. Arguably, preoccupation with the source of the offense may distract defenders and keep them from paying sufficiently close attention to the psychic arena at home where doctrines and opinions collide. It is within the souls of subphilosophic citizens that the founding opinions fundamental to the perpetuation of the regime hold sway, or gain strength, or insensibly crumble. How might these opinions be defended and secured against artful (or, for that matter, mindless) corruption by others? One way might be through the methods of confrontation and contention so dear to the hearts of dialectical theologians. Another, more engaging method might be to tell a story. The power of a historical narrative to shape and even alter opinions, to present vivid images of exemplary behavior or cautionary lessons: that was a possibility as present to Jefferson as to Fārābī.[6]

This mode of popular persuasion and instruction remains close to the level of received opinion, presenting a strong likely case without demonstrative argument. Yet it may and often does raise the question "Why?," and to that extent is not simply defensive and not necessarily conservative. Far from simply accepting the ancestral *because* it is old—the conservative stance par excellence—and thereby closing off anything even approaching theoretical inquiry, the recourse to history invites those so inclined and so able to wonder about the reasons and causes that led the forebears to think and act as they did. In seeking to recover those reasons, it enters, however tentatively, into a broader and more challenging field. Here is a chance to move beyond merely passive piety and a gratitude for ancestral efforts. By rising to the demands

6. See Fārābī, *The Book of Religion* (*Kitāb al-Millah*), sect. 2. The Arabic text is in *Alfarabi's Book of Religion and Related Texts* (*Kitāb al-Millah wa-Nuṣūṣ Ukhrā*), edited by Muhsin Mahdi (Beirut: Dar el-Machreq Publishers [Imprimerie Catholique], 1968), 45.9–24. See also the discussion of public education in Query 14 of Thomas Jefferson, *Notes on the State of Virginia*, edited by William Peden (Chapel Hill: University of North Carolina Press for the Institute of Early American History and Culture, 1954), 147–48.

and opportunities of thoughtful participation, the beneficiaries of today may themselves prove worthy, in turn, of the thanks of their successors.

Examination of the political science of Plato and of his follower Fārābī may disclose it to be more finely attuned to the nuances of statesmanship than is its avowedly more realistic contemporary replacement. Likewise, examination of the manner in which Burke, Lincoln, and Tocqueville retell the stories of their national revolutions may give added impetus to our looking beyond our now conventional categories. In each case the statesman begins by seeking to settle his public's mind about some distressing issue of the day. To do so he makes use of an old art at once poetic and philosophic, seductive and hectoring, adroit and naive. His defense of his regime is designed to stiffen the unsteady, rouse the drowsy, and meet the enemy on his own ground. Like the dialectical theology described by Fārābī, this political *kalām* is no shy and timid voice.

5

Burke's Muffled Oars

From first to last in his long career as a public man, Edmund Burke insists on a self-conscious scrutiny of one's *stance* when approaching questions of public policy. Ignorance, inexperience, myopia, closed-mindedness (whether prompted by self-satisfaction, indifference, or sloth): each rules out the chance that sound policy might be found and followed. As surely as "a great empire and little minds go ill together," so too might it be said more generally that the conduct of the public's business demands enlarged views both from the few charged with that business and from the many empowered to select them (*C* 1:509).[1] An electorate

1. There is as yet no complete edition of Burke's writings that meets present-day critical standards, but one is under way. All volume and page citations given here parenthetically are to *The*

that expects its representatives to behave like lapdogs will get what it deserves—creeping servility—not what it most needs. To rise above some "partial, narrow, contracted, pinched, occasional system," one utterly unfit for great objects of national concern, a people has first to attract and indulge the

---

Works of the Right Honourable Edmund Burke, 6 vols. (London: Henry G. Bohn, 1854–56). Where superior editions exist I have followed those texts but cited the Bohn edition's pagination. In the case of *A Philosophical Enquiry into the Origin of our Ideas of the Sublime and Beautiful*, the text quoted is that edited by James T. Boulton (Notre Dame, Ind.: University of Notre Dame Press, 1968). In the case of *Reflections on the Revolution in France*, the text quoted is that edited by William B. Todd (New York: Rinehart, 1959), which was followed as well by Conor Cruise O'Brien in his Pelican Classics edition (Baltimore: Penguin Books, 1968). In the case of *A Vindication of Natural Society*, the text quoted is that edited by Frank N. Pagano (Indianapolis: Liberty Classics, 1982). Burke's writings have been identified by the following abbreviations:

A	*An Appeal from the New to the Old Whigs* (1791)
AE	*Substance of the Speech on the Army Estimates* (1790)
B	*Speech at Bristol, previous to the Election* (1780)
C	*Speech on moving his Resolutions for Conciliation with America* (1775)
CM	*Observations on the Conduct of the Minority* (1793)
E-I	*Speech on the East-India Bill* (1783)
ER	*Speech on presenting . . . a plan for . . . the Economical Reformation of the Civil and other Establishments* (1780)
MNA	*Letter to a Member of the National Assembly* (1791)
NL	*A Letter . . . to a Noble Lord* (1796)
O	*Observations on a late Publication, intituled "The Present State of the Nation"* (1769)
R	*Reflections on the Revolution in France* (1790)
RR	*On the Reform of the Representation in the House of Commons* (1782)
SB	*A Philosophical Enquiry into the Origin of our Ideas of the Sublime and Beautiful* (1757, 1759)
T	*Speech on American Taxation* (1774)
TFA	*Thoughts on French Affairs* (1791)
V	*A Vindication of Natural Society* (1756, 1757)

right sort of men (*C* 1:457). Only by giving "confidence to their [representatives'] minds, and a liberal scope to their understandings," only by permitting representatives "to act upon a *very* enlarged view of things" will a people enable such independent-minded men to act with effect (*B* 2:130; see *ER* 2:66). But that of course presupposes that the legislative assembly is composed of individuals of "natural weight and authority," respectable in their own eyes and in those of their leaders, individuals of such situations and "such habits as enlarge and liberalize the understanding" (*R* 2:314). There is after all no substitute for "knowledge of mankind, . . . experience in mixed affairs, . . . a comprehensive connected view" of things (*R* 2:318).

In short, much depends upon what the would-be policymakers bring to their task. Foremost perhaps among their qualifications would be a healthy regard for facts and an equally healthy suspicion of theory. Burke encourages the impression that facts and theories are not merely distinct considerations, each entitled to its proper weight, but antonyms marking profoundly divergent stances toward human affairs. He usually begins sensibly enough by urging his audience to attend to the facts, to the record of experience. The character and situation of a people, their temper and expectations—more generally, "circumstances": these are the legislators' givens and hence should not be ignored or dismissed (*C* 1:456, 477, 479–80, 493; *R* 2:282). In absence of knowledge of the relevant facts, legislators are to proffer no advice: "I must see with mine own eyes, I must, in a manner, touch with my own hands" (*MNA* 2:548–49). Still less is moral judgment to be abstracted from circumstances (*A* 3:14).

Being granted this much, Burke presses his advantage. He for one "meddle[s] with no theory" (*C* 1:489). Neither will he be drawn into demarcating rights. "I do not enter into these metaphysical distinctions; I hate the very sound of them." These he would leave to the schools, the only place where they can be discussed with safety (*T* 1:432). It is less theory as such that Burke inveighs against than the theorizing frame of mind, just as it is not geometry or mathematics that he attacks when castigating those who seek "delusive geometrical accuracy in moral arguments" or who preclude prudence by treating "the lines of morality . . . like the ideal lines of mathematics" (*C* 1:501; *A* 3:16). Although "metaphysics" and "metaphysical" can often carry the tone of an undeleted obscenity in Burke's superheated prose, we do well to remember that his batteries are leveled against false or perverted philosophy. "I do not vilify theory and speculation— no, because that would be to vilify reason itself" (*RR* 6:148). Thus he expects a "civilized posterity" to distinguish the abuses wrought by fanatical pretenders to philosophy from the behavior of the genuine article. Philosophy along with religion he counts "the two most valuable blessings conferred upon us by the bounty of the universal Patron." He even goes so far as to hope that a calmer age will not retaliate upon "the speculative and inactive atheists of future times" (*R* 2:414).[2] Yet for all this, the problem in Burke's time is hardly the intolerance of an atheoretical public for the refinements of subtle thinkers but rather the reverse. Theory has so to speak taken the field of battle. There are few who would seek guidance from experience and choose to follow "nature,

2. Just as Burke is suspicious of a philosophy whose objective is something other than virtue itself, so too he distances himself philosophically from anything smacking of popular fury and governmental excess. He is more than ready to oppose wrath parading as justice, especially when it is fueled by scorn. See his impromptu and deeply felt expression of revulsion (on the floor of the House of Commons) provoked by a newspaper account of the pillorying and murderous abuse of two men convicted of "sodomitical practices," a crime that Burke regards as "of the most equivocal nature." *Parliamentary History of England* (London: T. C. Hansard), 11 Apr. 1780, vol. 21, cols. 388–90. See also his importuning letters and reflections on the bloody aftermath of the Gordon Riots (Bohn ed., 5:513–21). (I am indebted to Francis DuVinage for drawing my attention to these passages.)

which is wisdom without reflection, and above it," and those few—like Burke—are held in derision. Protest though they may that "we are guided not by the superstition of antiquarians, but by the spirit of philosophic analogy," the impulse among the knowing (and their unknowing followers) is to write this down to mindlessness (*R* 2:307).

It must be confessed that this misreading of Burke's intention is one he invites. He insists that Britain ought to govern America according to its peculiar nature and circumstances, "by no means according to mere general theories of government"; he insists that Parliament choose to abide by either "a profitable experience or a mischievous theory" (*C* 1:456, 496); he praises John Selden and "the other profoundly learned men" who drew up the Petition of Right for allowing their practical wisdom to supersede their theoretic science (*R* 2:306). "All the nakedness and solitude of metaphysical abstraction" draws his reactive fire (*R* 2:282), as he recoils from "the mazes of metaphysic sophistry" he detects in the arguments of Jacobins on both sides of the Channel. "I have nothing to say to the clumsy subtilty of their political metaphysics" (*R* 2:295, 331). The methods and results of such ingenious theorizing drive Burke into making studied, even perverse glorifications of what most folk would see as faults or even vices. Of this tactic, so much indulged in the *Reflections*, one may truly say that the stone rejected by enlightened builders is become his chief cornerstone: "Thanks to our sullen resistance to innovation, thanks to the cold sluggishness of our national character, we still bear the stamp of our forefathers. We have not (as I conceive) lost the generosity and dignity of thinking of the fourteenth century; nor as yet have we subtilized ourselves into savages" (*R* 2:358).

Burke accepts the mockery of his sophisticated opponents, even with relish, and dares to convert their contempt into an adornment. He answers burlesque with burlesque. The French alternative—that is to say, the alternative offered by disciples of Rousseau, Voltaire, and Helvétius (not those of Montesquieu)—is to sublime oneself into "an airy metaphysician," to become one of that lot of "metaphysical and alchemistical legislators," "to follow in their desperate flights the aëronauts of France" (*R* 2:455, 512, 517). To engage in such systematic doctrinairism, "to scorn all mediocrity—to engage for perfection—to proceed by the simplest and shortest course" is to play "a most desperate game" indeed (*A* 3:108–9; *R* 2:456).

For Burke the *philosophes*' curt dismissal of the tolerable in favor of the best bespeaks not only an abstract philanthropy but a profound ignorance of the foundations of political life. With them the past is an incubus, not an entailed inheritance; they would break the grip of habit rather than use it to advantage. Thus the inanities and incongruities of any long-lived regime are in their eyes only fit for ridicule and ripe for the rubbish heap. Burke takes special pains to establish that a strong regard for habitual modes need not be a commitment to the absurd (*RR* 6:147; *R* 2:307). Opposing, as always, ancient policy and practice to the speculations of innovators on both sides of the question, Burke claims to find "great, manly, and sure ground" (*T* 1:431). He looks to the British constitution as to an "oracle," a "treasury" of maxims and principles, and finds there the "healthy habit" that can preserve a people and its government from their most restless and intemperate impulses (*C* 1:483; *R* 2:298).

At bottom all governments find security in opinion, or in some "mixed system of opinion and sentiment," or in illusions "furnished from the wardrobe of a moral imagination" (*R* 2:288, 348–49). Those charged with the conduct of public affairs ought to be wary of deliberately or even inadvertently subverting those "allowed opinions which contribute so much to the public tranquility" (*C* 1:471; see *R* 2:288). In following "our old settled maxim, never entirely nor at once to depart from antiquity," the English act on "feelings still native and entire" (*R* 2:372, 358). Their theories, such as they are, derive from experience rather than precede it (*R* 2:442–43). That experience in turn confirms their feelings and reinforces their prejudices; it even leads Englishmen—"to take more shame to ourselves"—to cherish their prejudices *because* they are prejudices. "Prejudice renders a man's virtue his habit; and not a series of unconnected acts. Through just prejudice, his duty becomes a part of his nature" (*R* 2:359).

Yet simply to rely on prejudice and habit would be naive, even heedless. For in the course of time the familiar may come to seem banal; a yearning for change, a taste for adventure may lead a people to "become less sensible to a long-possessed benefit" and correspondingly more sanguine and less wary (*A* 3.12). Caught between the imprudence of contending fanatics, they lose a sense of proportion and come "to neglect those provisions, preparations, and precautions, which distinguish benevolence from imbecillity" (*R* 2:300, 312). They forget how furious and unbounded passions can be when fueled by speculation and "system" (*A* 3:99). They fail to recognize and take the measure of "the most important of all revolutions, . . . I mean a revolution in sentiments, manners, and moral opinions" (*R* 2:352). In turning a blind eye to the long-term consequences of new opinions, they remain oblivious (until too late) while a general demoralization and censure work their effects (*A* 3:81, 106; *RR* 6:152–53; *R* 2:296–97).

Notwithstanding his celebration of just prejudice, Burke clearly believes that speculative inquiries have their place. He never denies the contribution they may make to greater clarity and real improvements. Nor does he deny that in extreme situations "good men, finding everything already broken up, think it right to take advantage of the opportunity of such derangement" (*O* 1:259–60). But extreme cases are by definition atypical. It is an entirely different matter when "the cool Light of Reason" is gratuitously encouraged to expose the nakedness of old cherished opinions (*V* 1:48). There is even greater reason for drawing "a sacred veil" over the beginnings of all governments.

Time, in the origin of most governments, has thrown this mysterious veil over them; prudence and discretion make it necessary to throw something of the same drapery over more recent foundations. . . . But whatever necessity might hide or excuse or palliate, in the acquisition of power, a wise nation, when it has once made a revolution upon its own principles and for its own ends, rests there.[3]

When those who know better (and who have every self-interested motive to know better) act with "a sort of sportive acquiescence" and allow the people's habitual attachment to the constitution "to be brought into contempt before their faces," they err grievously in imagining themselves only uninvolved spectators of a farce (*A* 3:106–7).[4] Paradox, novelty, and surprise all have their charms. In the "Fairy Land of Philosophy," ingenuity dazzles the imagination and the mind doubts itself. The pleasing impressions linger on even after the supporting reasons are exploded. How might such a dissolving, deconstructive reason be engaged and countered? Only by "a painful, comprehensive Survey of a very complicated Matter," a survey demanding "a great Variety of Considerations." Nor is that all. In moving beyond commonplaces and in plumbing a profound subject, one must seek not only arguments but "new Materials of Argument, their Measures and their Method of Arrangements." In addition, all manner of people in the audience must in some fashion or

---

3. Speech in Opening the Impeachment of Warren Hastings, Second Day, 16 Feb. 1788, in *The Works of the Right Honorable Edmund Burke*, 9th ed., 12 vols. (Boston: Little, Brown, and Company, 1889), 9:401–2. See also the discussion of prescription in *R* 2:435.

4. Why then this constant harping upon revolutionary doctrines? "It is not easy to state for what good end, at a time like this, when the foundations of all ancient and prescriptive governments, such as ours, (to which people submit, not because they have chosen them, but because they are born to them,) are undermined by perilous theories, that Mr. Fox should be so fond of referring to those theories, upon all occasions, even though speculatively they might be true, which God forbid they should!" (*CM* 3:498)

other be reached (*V* 1:3–4). Thus with his first steps onto the public stage, Burke lays bare the problem he would have to confront throughout his life in developing a rhetoric in the service of his political *kalām*.

☾☽

Revolution has for Burke all the fascination of a cobra. He dares not take his eye off it. At the extreme would be those occasions of "public necessity, so vast, so clear, so evident, that they supersede all laws." He knows full well that no absolute case can be made for the ancestral. At some point "an inheritance of absurdity" can no longer pass muster as part of a liberal descent and be defended with a straight face. "There is a time when men will not suffer bad things because their ancestors have suffered worse." Antiquity must then justify itself, for "when the reason of old establishments is gone, it is absurd to preserve nothing but the burthen of them. This is superstitiously to embalm a carcass not worth an ounce of the gums that are used to preserve it" (*ER* 2:101, 64, 83; see *B* 2:158, *A* 3:101). At the same time, speaking as a member of his public, Burke categorically rules out "the very idea of the fabrication of a new government" and insists that all reform proceed upon "the principle of reference to antiquity." An awareness of the debt owed to the past works to moderate the impetuosity of the present life-renters (*R* 2:305, 308, 366–67). For all this, Burke admits that revolution may be the right and proper course for a people to follow; "but, with or without right, a revolution will be the very last resource of the thinking and the good." The administering of such extreme medicine must be left to those fitted by nature to make that judgment (*R* 2:304). And like extreme medicine, revolution ought not to be rendered commonplace. "This distemper of remedy, grown habitual, relaxes and wears out, by a vulgar and prostituted use, the spring of that spirit which is to be exerted on great occasions" (*R* 2:335–36). Even the most justifiable and most needful revolution exacts a high price. "It was long before the spirit of true piety and true wisdom, involved in the principles of the Reformation, could be depurated from the dregs and feculence of the contention with which it was carried through" (*B* 2:144–45; *A* 3:16).

Even reform and renovation, Burke's great alternatives to violent upheaval, fill him with anxiety. True politicians begin and end with a presumption in favor of what is. They change what they must, but always with a view to preserving as much as they can (*R* 2:427–28, 516). Above all they take care not to be the unwitting sappers of what they mean to secure. Thus they are alert never to confuse reform with innovation (*A* 3:38; *ER* 2:102; *AE* 3:274; *NL* 5:120). In practice this means, among other things, anticipating now in order to avoid worse later on, but not doing evil before it is done to you. It also means resisting the temptation, ever present in "hot reformations," to be thorough and to aim for a final solution. Perhaps one of the worst effects of fury is the disgust it generates for the idea on whose behalf it is exerted. Prudent reformers behave otherwise. By choosing instead to be patient and diffident, by taking in a longer perspective, and by saving some reform for later generations to accomplish, they show a becoming zeal and an equally becoming fear (*ER* 2:64–65; *R* 2:439–40; *A* 3:114). Such reformers will attend to the reach of the principles involved when contemplating any project for change. They dare not be surprised by unforeseen (or disingenuously concealed) consequences. "Doctrines limited in their present application, and wide in their general principles, are never meant to be confined to what they at first pretend" (*A* 3:98).

The actions of true lawgivers, then, are marked by an even timid circumspection.[5] They know that "a state without the means of some change is without the means of its conservation." But they know as well that lasting reform depends

5. "A politic caution, a guarded circumspection, a moral rather than a complexional timidity were among the ruling principles of our forefathers in their most decided conduct" (*R* 2:517).

upon a union of minds, something that only time can produce—and slowly, almost imperceptibly, at that (*R* 2:295, 439). Whether in forming an evolving Magna Charta for Hindostan, or in prudently easing a prejudiced English people into a disposition for justice toward Catholics, Burke is prepared to make slow beginnings, the better to gain "the advantage of a progressive experience" (*E-I* 2:179; *B* 2:158).

No small amount of art is required to achieve this balance of conservation and correction. How best to regenerate the deficient part of the constitution without simultaneously dissolving the entire social fabric (*R* 2:295)? For Burke the answer lies beyond the range of ordinary prudence and in what might be called the art of political camouflage. Rather than dismiss with a sneer the dilapidated remains of the old order, "a true politician always considers how he shall make the most of the existing materials of his country." In so doing he gives silent recognition to the insufficiency of human reason and preserves for the new a claim based on the prescription of the old. He avoids the folly of setting up a trade without a capital fund (*R* 2:428, 308–9; *MNA* 2:553). In practice this means making "the reparation as nearly as possible in the style of the building" (*R* 2:517). More than an aesthetic preference lies behind this injunction; whatever it is, it is not simply a love for uniformity.[6] Rather, Burke's consideration is to conceal the discontinuity as much as possible and to divert attention from the architects and builders. Not for him are the ornamental gardens of the French, whose very splendor proclaims the glory of their designers' and artisans' skills and mastery over nature. Burke's old building is rather like an English garden, varied, irregular, seemingly unpremeditated, fostering the pleasing delusion that this is how it has always been. In this context, artistic triumph consists less in heightening the sharp dis-

6. Calls prompted by such an infatuation only make Burke "feel a sort of nausea" (*O* 1:257).

tinction between nature and artifice than in thoroughly blur-
ring the difference.

Burke's use of history is governed by the same intent. As he
paddles his narrative through the troubled waters of the past,
one cannot but be aware of his use of muffled oars. He means
to make no waves. Rather than call attention to himself as a
theorist or to the historic role of other theorists of political
right, he would have us attribute much to the studied judgments of statesmen. He is, of course, in no position to deny
that on more than one occasion in Britain, "an irregular,
convulsive movement" has been resorted to so as to "throw
off an irregular, convulsive disease." But he presents such acts
of necessity in a kind of chiaroscuro. What is more, Burke
insists on drawing our attention to those statesmen's art of
concealment even while practicing it himself. "It is curious to
observe with what address this temporary solution of con-
tinuity is kept from the eye" (R 2:298, 292). Repeatedly he
emphasizes the integrity of the principle even as it is being
subjected to what he calls "a small and a temporary devia-
tion." Never was the legislature more tender of principle than
when it parted from it. This was as true in 1688–89, when
"the crown was carried somewhat out of the line in which it
had before moved," as in the series of bloody discontinuous
policies by which seventeenth-century England tried to sub-
due Ireland (R 2:291, 296; C 1:484). In all such extremities,
Burke argues, it is never a matter of all or nothing: indisputa-
bly sovereign power still subjects its will to moral restraints.
"That point being fixed, and laying fast hold of a strong
bottom, our speculations may swing in all directions without
public detriment, because they will ride with sure anchorage" (R 2:294; A 3:55).

It is safe to say that for Burke no less significant than *what*
the managers of the Glorious Revolution accomplished is
how they did it. Theirs is in that sense a double legacy well
worth retelling. Indeed, in the *Reflections* Burke purports to
do little more than "to repeat a very trite story, to recall to
your memory," "to call back our attention"—in short, to

restate common knowledge (*R* 2:291–92, 299). Far from embellishing the record or deepening the analysis, Burke disclaims any desire to be a better or a more thoughtful Whig than those who made the revolution or than those who in the years following the revolution had seen that free constitution "alive and in action" (*R* 2:294; *A* 3:44). In understanding that revolution as its principals did, one could not possibly confound it with either the Puritan Revolution or the French Revolution. Yet English partisans of the French did make such a mistaken association, and it is precisely this confounding that sets Burke in motion. His bitter and unrelenting attacks on the astonishing events in France are prompted above all by fear that the people of England might be captivated by "the newest Paris fashion of an improved liberty" being marketed by political theologians and theological politicians (*R* 2:290, 284, 299). In turning to the principles of the Glorious Revolution and the prudence of its managers, Burke seeks to lead his public back to safe anchorage.

The events of 1688–89 add up to that rarity—"an honest and necessary revolution." The "virtuous policy" of its managers entitles it to be called glorious and sets it apart as a model for others. Burke skirts the exact manner in which "a bad king with a good title" was replaced by the nation acting in a sort of defensive war. The subversion of the old ought rather to be viewed in the light of what follows. Judging the totality of 1688–89, then, it was a "very regular step," "a revolution, not made, but prevented." A kingdom without a king was preserved *as* a kingdom; in no essential was its constitution changed (*MNA* 2:527, 544; *R* 2:297; *A* 3:15, 45, 56; *AE* 3:279).[7]

7. The comforting neatness of Burke's account appears otherwise in modern scholarship where the decisive events are the actions of contending dynasts, not the ruminations of the Convention of 1689. As Robert Beddard explains, "The Revolution not only marked the triumph of William III over James II, and of Protestantism over Catholicism, it overthrew the principle of primogeniture by which

The true center of Burke's narrative, the idea on which he would have his audience focus their minds, is "the spirit of caution which predominated in the national councils" of the time. Obliged by "a grave and overruling necessity," the anxious leaders of the revolution did what they did with "infinite reluctance," being "totally adverse . . . from turning a case of necessity into a rule of law" (*R* 2:301, 291). Burke fairly glows with admiration at John Somers's "address" in concealing unsettling deeds and unsettling thoughts in "pious, legislative ejaculation" and "traditionary language."[8]

---

the crown had passed from one monarch to another since 1509." Furthermore, in evaluating the revolution's character one has to recall that in 1661 Parliament had "decreed it high treason to distinguish between the person and the office of king, as the Parliamentarian rebels had done in 1642. That is why to contemporary Englishmen the events of 1688–9 were truly revolutionary. In pressing his claim to the throne during King James's lifetime William and his supporters drew the forbidden distinction, which was expressly revolutionary, between the institution of monarchy, which they were careful to preserve, and the person of the monarch, whom they unceremoniously discarded. The law of England did not countenance the forcible substitution of one dynast for another, such as had occurred." Robert Beddard, "The Unexpected Whig Revolution of 1688," in *The Revolutions of 1688: The Andrew Browning Lectures, 1988*, edited by Robert Beddard (Oxford: Clarendon Press, 1991), 94, 96. For other instances where Burke's account of 1688–89 is "highly selective in its omission of facts, methods, and consequences" see Peter J. Stanlis, *Edmund Burke: The Enlightenment and Revolution* (New Brunswick, N.J.: Transaction Publishers, 1991), 242–43.

8. The adroitness of Somers and his allies, many of whom "adhered still to the left-wing political and religious principles of Shaftesbury's 'first' Whigs," was even greater than Burke's account would lead one to suspect. See Lois G. Schwoerer, "The Role of Lawyers in the Revolution of 1688–89," in *Die Rolle der Juristen bei der Entstehung des modernen Staates*, edited by Roman Schnur (Berlin: Duncker & Humblot, 1986), 478, 483–84, 487–92.

In their act of settling the succession of the crown, Parliament "threw a politic, well-wrought veil over every circumstance tending to weaken the rights, which in the meliorated order of succession they meant to perpetuate; or which might furnish a precedent for any future departure from what they had then settled for ever" (*R* 2:292–93). Doubtless Burke runs risks in lifting that veil. In making his public conscious of the camouflaging arts practiced by his model statesmen, he might expect comparable sharp-sightedness to be directed toward him as well. For does not Burke adhere, as religiously as the parliamentarians and lawyers of 1689, to "the form of sound words" (*C* 1:491; *A* 3:40)?[9] Yet Burke, like his models, distinguishes public from private inquiry. Public homage to time-hallowed language does not exclude from private discussions "such terms of art as may serve to conduct an inquiry for which none but private persons are responsible" (*A* 3:40). Even while veiling some harsh necessities, Burke in his individual and private capacity persists "in speculating on what has been done, or is doing, on the public stage; in any place antient or modern" (*R* 2:280–81).

It is no less curious to observe how, in discussions of extreme situations, Burke lifts with one hand the veil his other hand is lowering. In this respect most especially he sets himself apart from those modern adherents of conservatism who claim him as their spiritual forebear. Needless to say, he is wary of indulging in casuistry for the sheer pleasure of it; "the very habit of stating these extreme cases is not very laudable or safe" (*A* 3:81). Yet despite himself he must admit that there are horrendous situations when it might be hard to discriminate the best men from the worst, moments when "the statues of Equity and Mercy might be veiled" (*MNA*

9. See, for example, Burke's resolutions for conciliation with the American colonies, laid down in "the language of your own ancient acts of Parliament." "What the law has said, I say. In all things else I am silent. I have no organ but for her words. This, if it be not ingenious, I am sure is safe" (*C* 1:490–91; see also 489, 499).

2:533; *R* 2:406). Truth to tell, we find consolation in the punishment of real tyrants, and we even abate our indignation against them somewhat when they in turn punish other exceedingly vicious people (*R* 2:355, 414–15). With candor and caution so much at odds, where can we find those guidelines by which true politicians might govern their speech?

(( ))

This tension at work within Burke's soul manifests itself as an important theme in his political science. With so much of his substantive policy directed toward conservation and tilted against the spirit of change, one would expect as a matter of course that his byword should be caution. Yet for all its plausibility, such an assessment is incomplete.[10] In an early work, *A Vindication of Natural Society*, Burke shows how fully he grasps the power and attraction of a commitment to the unqualified pursuit of truth. Adopting the persona of a late noble writer—worldly wise, weary, and writing privately to a young lord just entering onto the larger public stage—Burke presents a telling and hilarious portrait of a dedicated man of theory.[11] With the old lord it is all or nothing: anything is better than "an inconsistent Chimaera and Jumble of Philosophy and vulgar Prejudice." This fearless dissector is unconcerned "how near the Quick our Instruments may come." Affecting to be "a plain man," he speaks his mind. He disdains to gauge a proposition's truth or falsity by its apparent consequences, viewing such a no-

10. The reverse situation might obtain as well; " 'Caute' was the inscription of Spinoza's signet." Leo Strauss, *Persecution and the Art of Writing* (Glencoe, Ill.: Free Press, 1952), 180.

11. In my reading, the whole of the *Vindication of Natural Society* is wildly ironical. Burke himself is nowhere to be seen (is he the aging parody of Bolingbroke, or the anonymous editor?)—and hence everywhere.

tion as both absurd and blasphemous. His cry is the *philosophe*'s equivalent of "Damn the torpedoes! Full speed ahead!" (*V* 1:33-34, 21, 6, 8). The entire portrait is absurd. Avowedly avoiding "a Parade of Eloquence," the old lord wallows in hyperbole; he uses metaphor, then ostentatiously casts it aside and turns to simile; disdaining to address the vulgar and their vulgar passions, he openly crafts his calculation to work more upon the young lord's feelings than on his judgment (*V* 1:17–18, 34, 6). Yet even Burke's noble writer, caricature though he is, at least pays tribute to the need for caution. His commitment to truth-speaking, he would have us believe, is measured. The example of democratic Athens teaches that the truth is not to all men welcome; there are political reasons for holding back. "Atheism and Treason may be the Names given in *Britain*, to what would be Reason and Truth if asserted of *China*." Even in more private circumstances—like those that purportedly surround this juvenile production[12]—one dare not be heedless of audience. ". . . I know to whom I am speaking, for I am satisfied that Reasons are like Liquors, and there are some of such a Nature as none but strong Heads can bear" (*V* 1:29, 32, 36, 33).

In these lines, I believe, we hear an echo of Burke himself. He for one is never heedless of audience, even (or perhaps especially) when he seems most in the grip of some overwhelming rhetorical fancy. His passion; his intimidating arsenal of figures of speech; his rhetorical voice, which at times sounds almost about to crack—all these incline us to view him as being carried away and hence unconvincing. In arguing for moderation he often turns immoderate. These are not only good causes; they are *his* causes. His weighty cautions,

12. Burke's fiction highlights this. See in the "Advertisement" to the first edition (1756) of the *Vindication*: "As it is probable the Noble Writer had no Design that it should ever appear in Publick, this will account for his having kept no Copy of it, and consequently, for its not appearing amongst the rest of his Works" (Pagano ed., 97).

impressive as they are, cry to be balanced against his zeal. We hear him clearly enough urging a method that accords well with our natural limits. "We must make use of a cautious, I had almost said, a timorous method of proceeding. We must not attempt to fly, when we can scarcely pretend to creep." Nonetheless, there are moments when decorum yields to duty, and caution must give way. Some circumstances call for prudent reticence, others for prudent speaking (*SB* 1:50; *C* 1:453; *R* 2:284).

Burke speaks out often enough; more dubious, however, is whether his speech is all that measured. A few examples must suffice. Moderate defenses of "one of the great bad men of the old stamp (Cromwell)" and of large proprietors are followed by a discussion of the utility of religion not only for the lowly but for the high and mighty. The latter are noted for "the stench of their arrogance and presumption"; they exhibit a "fat stupidity and gross ignorance concerning what imports men most to know" (*R* 2:321, 324–25, 373–74). Burke confesses himself inclined (from a certain point of view) "forcibly to rescue" the many unhappy wretches who toil from dawn to dark, condemned to gratify the insatiable demands of the few (*R* 2:431–32; *V* 1:44–45). If ever a group needed liberation, it would be these far more than the monks whom the French revolutionaries have seen fit to "free." But Burke's concern for the interests and well-being of the majority does not encompass the notion that the majority ought itself to predominate. The idea of majority rule, now so habitual to Burke's audience as to be mistaken generally for "a law of our original nature," is disclosed by Burke to be "one of the most violent fictions of positive law that ever has been or can be made on the principles of artificial incorporation" (*A* 3:82–83).

Such examples, among many others, give added meaning to his proud assertion that he, Edmund Burke, stands for something. Addressing complaints and charges raised by his constituents in Bristol, he asks them to remember once more I do not mean to extenuate or excuse. Why should I, when the things charged are among those upon which I found all my reputation? What would be left to me, if I myself was the man, who softened, and blended, and diluted, and weakened, all the distinguishing colours of my life, so as to leave nothing distinct and determinate in my whole conduct? (*B* 2:134)

But taking a stand and adhering to it do not in any way require unmodulated speech or uniform emphasis. Quite to the contrary. "The *purpose* for which the abuses of government are brought into view forms a very material consideration in the mode of treating them. The complaints of a friend are things very different from the invectives of an enemy" (*A* 3:38). In that modulation and adaptation to circumstances lie both Burke's apparent inconsistency and his political art.

The question of a politician's consistency, especially where a long career is under scrutiny, is so commonplace as hardly to warrant comment. Opponents latch onto some divergence and hope to make it into a telling point. Much rarer is the case where the politician himself elevates consistency to a matter of honor and even self-definition. What is there to crow about? In some respects this issue is forced upon Burke by virtue of his prominence in the British debates over the American and French revolutions. But in other respects his consistency is an issue pressed by Burke himself. "I believe," he says (speaking of himself in the third person), "if he could venture to value himself upon anything, it is on the virtue of consistency that he would value himself the most." This proud assertion presupposes a distinction "between a difference in conduct under a variation of circumstances and an inconsistency in principle" (*A* 3:24, 27). In the realm of principle, he insists, he has long known where he stands and has stood there firmly. Early on, Burke has grasped "the necessity of forming some fixed ideas." Consistency in an individual bespeaks some inner ballast, something that preserves him from "being blown about by every wind of fashionable doctrine." Lacking that ballast, that principled center, one falls under the spell of fashion and into the habit of "tampering, the odious vice of restless and unstable minds" (*C* 1:451, 491). Thus Burke demands of himself what his constituents have every right to expect: that he (and not only he) be "a pillar of the state, and not a weathercock" (*B* 2:138). When he urges a return to the ancient policy and practice of the kingdom, it is so as to avoid "the evils of inconstancy and versatility, ten thousand times worse than those of obstinacy and the blindest prejudice" (*C* 1:489; *R* 2:367–68).

The recurring theme of Burke's *kalām* is that of return. He affects to speak only the primitive language of the law, to walk in the steps of his ancestors, and to subordinate his will to their experience and wisdom. Of course, that past is not nearly as unambiguous as Burke makes it out to be. Even the name of the Glorious Revolution evokes very different notions of what had transpired not so long ago and what it signified.[13] Yet that observation in a sense misses Burke's point. It is not the transparent or unambiguous character of each and every element of the past that matters so much as our awareness of the past's continuing relevance, weight, and dignity as a point of reference. The great and persisting danger—whether in questions of domestic reform; relations with America, Ireland, and India; or response to the overthrow of the *ancien régime*—is the present-mindedness and narrow focus of the shapers and conductors of public policy. Lacking even a yearning for a comprehensive view of the whole, they fall easily into improvisation while indulging their taste for short measures. Burke, in contrast, insists that "whether it be too much or too little, whatever I have done has been general and systematic" (*NL* 5:125).

13. See H. T. Dickinson, "The Eighteenth-Century Debate on the 'Glorious Revolution,' " *History: The Journal of the Historical Association*, n.s. 61, no. 201 (Feb. 1976): 28–45.

He can only "preserve consistency by varying his means to secure the unity of his end" (R 2:518). Each of the urgent issues of the day might be thought of as evidence of some distortion or distemper in the larger scheme of things. Exaggeration calls forth an equal and opposite exaggeration; whatever is most in jeopardy requires then and there the most vigorous defense.

> As any one of the great members of this constitution happens to be endangered, he that is a friend to all of them chooses and presses the topics necessary for the support of the part attacked, with all the strength, the earnestness, the vehemence, with all the power of stating, of argument, and of coloring, which he happens to possess and which the case demands. He is not to embarrass the minds of his hearers, or to incumber or overlay his speech, by bringing into view at once (as if he were reading an academic lecture) all that may and ought, when a just occasion presents itself, to be said in favor of the other members. At that time they are out of the court; there is no question concerning them. (A 3:25)

Politics, even under a stable and equable constitution, seem never at any moment to be at rest. The dynamics of political life preclude drowsy inattention. Rather, they call for defenders who can be both cool and warm. Burke's speeches bear witness to his exceptional skill and perseverance. They display as well an art without which "closet philosophy" would remain only that and zealous philosophy would reign unchecked.

Lincoln's Revolution

By the time Abraham Lincoln first finds his way to the public podium, the traditional objects of American political celebration have been much altered. In the beginning, and especially to the east of the Hudson, the Lord had been praised by governors no less than by clerics. Both knew whence all blessings flowed and were intent that the public at large never lose sight of that source. Later, the controversies that lead at last to revolution and independence lay greater stress on English law and institutions, the rightful inheritance of a free people. To laud this legacy is at once to justify the struggle and to condemn the corruption and heartlessness of an unfeeling imperious mother. Next, a free America, with a future as unbounded as the very land, offers itself as a new topic fit for orators and poets. But in congratulating themselves for their land, their institutions, their separate and equal station among the nations of the earth, Americans become great self-flatterers. Full of themselves, they are in no mood to listen to European visitors complain about boorish complacency and absurd puffery.

The European caricature is not entirely unfair. By the time it is Lincoln's turn to begin raising his voice among his fellow citizens, egregious self-celebration is a staple of American oratory. It is astonishing that he makes himself heard in such a congratulatory clamor, for he speaks in a different key. To be sure, Lincoln has no principled objection to praising America to the Americans. But his conception of the praise-worthy in America is singular, and in the future tense: Americans will have reason to think well of themselves only after learning to think critically of themselves. In the meantime, one does not have to be a European observer, just a far-seeing American, to understand that the American people's self-satisfaction is the greatest obstacle to a well-deserved pride in themselves. In a time and place where thousands heap whole-sale flattery (and wholesale damnation) upon uncritical millions, Lincoln's is a voice apart.

( )

No aspiring politician needs to be told that there is a public pulse to be taken, and no halfway competent politician needs to grope for long to take it. Lincoln is more than halfway competent. He understands from the outset and with perfect clarity that the realm of politics is the realm of opinion. He sees that any speaker who would induce a people to hold a critical opinion of itself must first induce it to trust and have a good opinion of himself. But it will presumably not trust or have a good opinion of one who criticizes the opinions it holds dear. It would seem, then, that in order to gain a hearing for his critical, nonflattering speech, a speaker must first dissemble his critical opinions and flatter his audience, thus exacerbating the very sickness he wishes to cure.

Lincoln escapes his dilemma in a manner worthy of study.

He flatters the people and gains their trust, not by catering to their present noncritical opinions of themselves and their affairs, but by bringing them with him, as equals somehow, into the problem of public opinion as such. He takes them into his confidence and makes them his partners in seeking a solution for the problem of popular government. And in this he succeeds. Not the least of Lincoln's extraordinary political achievements is his success in making general an awareness of the problem of public opinion—his nurturing of an opinion about the signal importance of opinion. A greater achievement, yet impossible without the first, is his persuading many American people to criticize and repudiate the many base opinions about political right and prudence that their base flatterers would have them basely cling to. His *kalām* is directed against the enemy within.

Lincoln's beginning point is the recognition that the basis of any government, "and particularly of those constituted like ours," lies in the attachment of the people to their government's laws and institutions (*SW* 1:31; *CW* 1:111).[1] That affection, in turn, although usually arising out of an untroubled confidence or habit, can nonetheless be alienated. The unspoken attachment of a silent multitude can suddenly and terribly show itself to be conditional, evanescent. Thus, far from being something to be presumed, the positive engagement of private sentiment and public structures has rather to be cultivated, nourished, and, in the last analysis, earned. The first fact is that "our government rests in public opinion. Whoever can change public opinion, can change

1. The volume and page locations of all quotations in this essay are cited parenthetically in the text. References are to two editions, separated by a semicolon. The first reference is to Abraham Lincoln, *Speeches and Writings*, edited by Don E. Fehrenbacher, 2 vols. (New York: Library of America, 1989); the title is abbreviated *SW*. The second is to *The Collected Works of Abraham Lincoln*, edited by Roy P. Basler et al., 9 vols. (New Brunswick, N.J.: Rutgers University Press, 1953–55); the title is abbreviated *CW*.

the government, practically just so much" (*SW* 1:385; *CW* 2:385). That public opinion might as readily be thought of as "a public sentiment" or as a public will that "springs from the two elements of moral sense and self-interest" (*SW* 1:402; *CW* 2:409). Politicians no less than policies are to be gauged by public sentiment: "In this age, and this country, public sentiment is every thing. *With* it, nothing can fail; *against* it, nothing can succeed" (*SW* 1:493; *CW* 2:552–53). But by the same token, politicians no less than policies are to be gauged by their effect *upon* public sentiment. When someone of influence molds public sentiment, he "goes deeper than he who enacts statutes or pronounces decisions. He makes statutes and decisions possible or impossible to be executed" (*SW* 1:525; *CW* 3:27).

Rather than remain the tacit understanding in a politician's private calculations, the shaping of public sentiment itself becomes, thanks to Lincoln, a subject of public reflection and debate. His insistence on addressing the " 'central idea' in our political public opinion" (*SW* 1:385; *CW* 2:385) also enables or rather compels others to perceive how a "mighty, deep seated power . . . somehow operates on the minds of men, exciting and stirring them up in every avenue of society—in politics, in religion, in literature, in morals, in all the manifold relations of life" (*SW* 1:805; *CW* 3:310).

Lincoln's concern with public opinion differs from the radicalizing summons of a principled politician. A William Lloyd Garrison, a John C. Calhoun, even an Alexis de Tocqueville, might single out some central idea as the shaper of social thoughts and ways. Lincoln goes further and deeper. He offers more than a dissecting tool of analysis or a call to arms. Lincoln contends that "no policy that does not rest upon some philosophical public opinion can be permanently maintained" (*SW* 2:136; *CW* 4:17). In raising this concern at all, he in effect attempts to mold and create a philosophically grounded public opinion. Where others see a public wanting in belief, Lincoln sees a public also wanting in understanding. Others would rouse their people to subscribe to some principle or article of faith. Lincoln does too; but beyond that, he strives to get as many as possible to pause, to reflect on the place and importance of true opinion in their collective lives.

Lincoln's analysis of the crisis of his time leads him to understand that it is no less the crisis of popular government itself. Only a general clarity about the conditions of popular government and only a greater awareness of the role of public opinion within it can enable the Americans to recover their balance and find themselves. Failing that, they will remain victims of their delusions and deluders.

If public opinion is the bedrock on which institutions and policies might be erected, it is also a formidable and omnipresent constraint on the hopes and dreams of theoretic politicians. "The universal *sense* of mankind, on any subject, is an argument, or at least an *influence* not easily overcome" (*SW* 1:85; *CW* 1:275). Confronting such opinions demands not only persistence and adroitness—qualities common enough to fanatics as well—but a genuine and cautious respect for limits, both one's own and those of others. In impinging on the deepest feelings of the people, politicians stir matters not to be trifled with. From early on Lincoln has understood and publicly acknowledged (as in his handbill replying to charges of infidelity) that no one "has the right . . . to insult the feelings, and injure the morals, of the community in which he may live" (*SW* 1:140; *CW* 1:382). Still less can a "statesman" feign indifference to some "great and durable element of popular action" (*SW* 1:346; *CW* 2:282). Indeed, the same may be said of more contentious and problematic popular sentiments. Whether a particular prejudice "accords with justice and sound judgment, is not the sole question, if indeed, it is any part of it. A universal feeling, whether well or ill-founded, can not be safely disregarded" (*SW* 1:316; *CW* 2:256).

All this, to repeat, bespeaks a need for caution, not a mindless acceptance. Lincoln is far, very far, from the resigned man of sorrows, controlled by events, that he is sometimes portrayed as being. His reentry into national politics is triggered by the crisis over the Kansas-Nebraska Act of 1854. No small part of his resolve to do battle comes from his perception of the injury that the mere passage of that legislation has already inflicted on a fragile, vulnerable public sentiment. Underlying the entire political system of the United States is a "spirit of mutual concession—that spirit which first gave us the constitution, and which has thrice saved the Union" (*SW* 1:335; *CW* 2:272). Who now, after the effectual repeal of the Missouri Compromise, could ever again put their trust in such mutual accommodations? More immediately, how might one account for so startling a reversal and repudiation? This latter question is the great device with which Lincoln seeks to arouse and redirect public opinion. In the course of doing so he succeeds in reversing the trajectories of both his own and Stephen A. Douglas's fortunes.

Central to Lincoln's purpose is his effort to impress upon the public mind the realization that "on the question of liberty, as a principle, we are not what we have been." The spirit that drove "the political slaves of King George" to wrest freedom for themselves and to desire a peaceful end to the enslavement of others has "itself become extinct, with the *occasion*, and the *men* of the Revolution" (*SW* 1:359; *CW* 2:318). Americans are abandoning the equality of men, that original "central idea" of American public opinion "from which all its minor thoughts radiate" (*SW* 1:385; *CW* 2:385). What is more, those keenest on overturning and replacing that principle have the audacity to deny publicly that any such reversal has taken place. The untruth buried in Chief Justice Taney's discreetly disingenuous assumption—"that the public estimate of the black man is more favorable *now* than it was in the days of the Revolution" (*SW* 1:396; *CW* 2:403)—is being asserted more brazenly by members of Congress. Thus John Pettit of Indiana, without a word of rebuke from "the forty odd Nebraska Senators who sat present and heard him," could pronounce the Declaration of Independence "a self-evident lie" (*SW* 1:339; *CW* 2:275). And Stephen

Douglas can maintain in effect "that negroes are not men—have no part in the declaration of Independence— . . . that liberty and slavery are perfectly consistent—indeed, necessary accompaniments—that for a strong man to declare himself the *superior* of a weak one, and thereupon enslave the weak one, is the very *essence* of liberty—the most sacred right of self-government" (*SW* 1:493–94; *CW* 2:553). Here is the "central idea of the Democratic party" under Douglas's leadership (*SW* 1:741; *CW* 3:256); under his influence "a vast change in . . . Northern public sentiment" has been effected in but a few years (*SW* 2:66; *CW* 3:444). It is a bitter irony that those who might rightly claim political descent from Jefferson have "nearly ceased to breathe his name everywhere" (*SW* 2:18; *CW* 3:375).

Lincoln presents Douglas's "Nebraskaism in its abstract purity" as a policy designed "to educate and mold public opinion to 'not care whether slavery is voted up or voted down' " (*SW* 1:416, 418; *CW* 2:451, 453). By "*impressing* the 'public heart' to *care* nothing about it" (*SW* 1:433; *CW* 2:467), Douglas is securing the "gradual and steady debauching of public opinion" (*SW* 2:56–57; *CW* 3:423). Coming from a man of great influence, Douglas's "bare opinion" goes far to fix that of others. "The susceptable young hear lessons from him, such as their fathers never heared when they were young" (*SW* 1:493; *CW* 2:553). The struggles, then, against Nebraskaism, against Douglas's "don't care" policy, against his insidious interpretation of popular sovereignty, are all presented by Lincoln as so many efforts to recover an earlier, authentic public opinion. Should Douglas's new heretical doctrines succeed in "penetrating the human soul" (*SW* 1:527; *CW* 3:29), there is little hope that slavery may be contained or that the public mind may once again come to "rest in the belief that it is going to its end" (*SW* 2:37; *CW* 3:406). To persuade his contemporaries that such an act of political recollection and recovery is both possible and desirable is the greatest challenge Lincoln faces until the coming of the war.

(( ))

As with his treatment of public sentiment, Lincoln chooses to make persuasion an explicit theme. To succeed in persuading, a speaker or writer has to come to terms with prevailing modes of thought, especially where these are reinforced by "interest, fixed habits, or burning appetites." These passionate involvements may be worked for good or for ill, but in no case are they to be ignored or despised. Thus it is futile to expect humankind at large to sacrifice now for the sake of generations yet unborn. "Posterity has done nothing for us; and theorise on it as we may, practically we shall do very little for it, unless we are made to think, we are, at the same time, doing something for ourselves." This understanding, according to Lincoln, informs the "more enlarged philanthropy" of the Washington Temperance Society (*SW* 1:85–86; *CW* 1:275–76). Less benign by far is the passion-driven misanthropy that can reduce the black man to a being intermediate to the white man and the crocodile. Here public passion is being worked so as to "still further brutalize the negro, and to bring public opinion to the point of utter indifference whether men so brutalized are enslaved or not" (*SW* 2:139–40; *CW* 4:20). Here too, as elsewhere, the public's passions are being catered to through use of ingenious falsehood and sophism. In this manner the unspeakable is concealed, "sugar-coated," and rendered plausible; the public mind is debauched and drugged (*SW* 2:138–39, 255; *CW* 4:19, 433).

For one engrossed in public affairs, the passion-driven preferences of the people must thus remain a matter of continuing concern and interest. However one views those particular passions—as something to be used or deflected, or even as something to be replaced and transcended—it is these passions that the politician must first somehow reach and affect. In this task the preeminent instrument of action is the politician's power of persuasion. Yet it is striking that so great a master of persuasive speech as Lincoln should insist on the limitations of such speech and thus also on the limits of politics. He understands the grip of mere fashion on ordinary behavior, "the strong inclination each of us feels to do as we see all our neighbors do" (*SW* 1:88; *CW* 1:277). He knows that "the plainest print cannot be read through a gold eagle" (*SW* 1:403; *CW* 2:409). He knows as well that it will not do to ignore a niggling charge, for although "it is no great thing, . . . yet the smallest are often the most difficult things to deal with" (*SW* 1:624; *CW* 3:135).

All this bespeaks a kind of modesty or perhaps realism when assessing politicians' effectiveness on their chosen fields of engagement. And yet in seeking to ground public opinion anew, Lincoln's objectives are hardly modest and certainly not timid. With the fading of public memories, with the dying-off of the men of '76—those impassioned embodiments of the revolution and its principles—Lincoln's generation has due warning that the temple of liberty "must fall, unless we, their descendants, supply their places with other pillars, hewn from the solid quarry of sober reason. Passion has helped us; but can do so no more. It will in future be our enemy" (*SW* 1:35–36; *CW* 1:115). Henceforth the politics of freedom must rest on the persuasiveness of reason.[2]

There is abundant evidence that Lincoln does indeed act on this estimate of his, and the American people's, situation. He takes it for granted that he will be held to account for positions he has adopted earlier and elsewhere, that "all the reading and intelligent men in the community would see them [in print] and know all about my opinions" (*SW* 1:703; *CW* 3:221). Similarly, he holds the opinions of his opponents to public accounting. They will need "a far better argument than a mere sneer to show to the minds of intelligent men" that they are not responsible for the necessary implications of their pronouncements (*SW* 1:715; *CW* 3:232). The ultimate political judge will be, has to be, a thinking public: "I never

2. That this is at least an overstatement is attested to by the lines that follow and form Lincoln's peroration: a heady, passionate appeal for the use of sober reason.

despair of sustaining myself before the people upon any measure that will stand a full investigation" (*SW* 1:42; *CW* 1:147).

Yet this confidence, which Lincoln articulates at the very outset of his political career and to which he holds firm till death, dare not be read as the manifesto of a *philosophe*. For although Lincoln loves a demonstrative proof as much as any man in public life, he holds no illusions as to its sufficiency either before the jury box or on the hustings. A widespread public opinion heavily discounts the pronouncements of "Preachers, Lawyers, and hired agents." "They are supposed to have no sympathy of feeling or interest, with those very persons whom it is their object to convince and persuade" (*SW* 1:81; *CW* 1:272). It is commonplace to write these types off as self-servers, especially when they assume high moral ground in denouncing and dictating to their erring fellow-citizens. Is it any surprise that the latter are "slow, *very slow*, . . . to join the ranks of their denouncers, in a hue and cry against themselves"? To expect otherwise is to anticipate what can never be—a reversal of human nature itself. This much at least is given: "that 'a drop of honey catches more flies than a gallon of gall.' So with men." Lincoln insists that "the great high road" to a man's reason has first to be gained, not assumed or commanded or despised. The ethos of the speaker has first to be established as that of a friend. Failing that, "tho' your cause be naked truth itself, transformed to the heaviest lance, harder than steel, and sharper than steel can be made, and tho' you throw it with more than Herculean force and precision, you shall no more be able to pierce him, than to penetrate the hard shell of a tortoise with a rye straw" (*SW* 1:83; *CW* 1:273).

Here, then, is a universal truth that informs and undergirds Lincoln's exertions on behalf of a politics of reason. His repeated appeal is of course to thoughtfulness. "I take it that I have to address an intelligent and reading community, who will peruse what I say, weigh it, and then judge . . ." (*SW* 1:704; *CW* 3:222). He tells the audience he shares with Douglas at

Galesburg that he is "willing and anxious that they should consider [the candidates' competing views] fully—that they should turn it about and consider the importance of the question, and arrive at a just conclusion." They should "decide, and rightly decide" the fundamental question concerning the extension of slavery before adopting any particular policy (*SW* 1:721; *CW* 3:236–37). Yet this appeal to deliberation will only be heeded if it is seen as coming from a friend, from one of their own. By drawing on a common heritage, the heritage of the revolution, and by casting himself as but one of a multitude of beneficiaries in common, Lincoln strives to find the high road to his public's reason. Happily, his need to persuade leads him to the plausible source of the very principles he would espouse. The revolution, as Lincoln conceives or reconceives it, makes him at one with his audience and points them all in common toward the practical policy that conforms to his understanding of justice.

( )

Within the context of the struggle over the expansion of slavery, Lincoln attempts to redirect his contemporaries' thoughts back to the revolution. His immediate aim is that they see afresh who they have been and what they are about. With recollection will come clarity, and with clarity, right action. In all of this Lincoln studiously avoids any suggestion that he is innovating, let alone improving on what earlier generations have wrought. The very language he favors in speaking of the founders' handiwork—the "legacy bequeathed us" (*SW* 1:28; *CW* 1:108), their "inestimable boon" (*SW* 2:264; *CW* 4:482)—reinforces the thought that the actions most becoming for latter-day Americans are of preserving and giving thanks. It might appear that with the greater work already accomplished, lesser men could now settle down to tasks better adapted to *their* talents.

Yet in fact Lincoln argues no such thing. For while his praise of the revolution and of the revolutionaries is predictably full, his estimate of that legacy is hardly simple or unmixed. There is, to begin with, no evading the fact that "the noblest of cause[s]" drew on some of the unloveliest human traits: the people's "deep rooted principles of *hate*, and the powerful motive of *revenge*" (*SW* 1:35; *CW* 1:114). Further, for all the revolution's "glorious results, past, present, and to come, it had its evils too. It breathed forth famine, swam in blood and rode on fire." It exacted a harsh human price, leaving in its wake orphans, widows, and a suppressed Tory minority (*SW* 1:89, 167; *CW* 1:278, 438–39).

Nor is that all. To be sure, the revolution's central proposition—the capability of a people to govern themselves—can no longer be treated as a matter of doubt. Its truth has been demonstrated in practice; the once "undecided experiment" is now understood to be a success (*SW* 1:33–34; *CW* 1:113). Yet the work remains strikingly incomplete. Bereft of its "noble ally," a complementary moral revolution, the grander goal of "our political revolution of '76" still lies beyond reach. The envisioned universal liberty of humankind demands not only the release of "every son of earth" from the oppressor's grip but also the breaking of the fiercer bondage of reason to human appetite and passion. No, the revolution can hardly be said to have run its course (*SW* 1:89–90; *CW* 1:278–79).

Nowhere is its incompleteness more evident than in the continuing debate over slavery. Lincoln repeatedly urges his countrymen to look back, "away back of the constitution, in the pure fresh, free breath of the revolution" (*SW* 1:309; *CW* 2:249). From that vantage point they may come to see both the promise of the revolution *and* its disappointment. A clue, for Lincoln, lies in Jefferson's having introduced into "a merely revolutionary document, an abstract truth, applicable to all men and all times" (*SW* 2:19; *CW* 3:376). Lincoln confesses to having long thought that this revolutionary struggle "must have been something more than common," "something even more than National Independence" (*SW* 2:209; *CW* 4:236). The object in view was not that eighteenth-century Americans achieve parity with eighteenth-century

British subjects "in their own oppressed and *unequal* condition," but rather "the progressive improvement in the condition of all men everywhere" (*SW* 1:399–400; *CW* 2:407). It was that expectation which sustained those who endured the miseries of the struggle: "they were cheered by the future" (*SW* 2:355; *CW* 5:373). It was that very expectation, now understood as "the principle of the REVOLUTION," which gave rise to those systems of gradual emancipation that the states had adopted in the closing decades of the preceding century (*SW* 1:342; *CW* 2:278). In the light of that history, and in view of the prosperity that attended the free states' having acted on the principle that "every man can make himself," it is simply absurd to pretend (as Douglas does) that these maxims of free government can be treated as indifferent matters. "No—we have an interest in the maintenance of the principles of the Government, and without this interest, it is worth nothing" (*SW* 1:379; *CW* 2:364).

In casting Douglas as the chief villain of the piece, Lincoln is responding particularly to the Democrat's attempt to establish historical credentials for his own policy. By denying or finessing the tension between original intent and current practice, Douglas is in effect erasing the disturbing memory that might impel an erring people to recover and reform. "Judge Douglas is going back to the era of our Revolution, and to the extent of his ability, muzzling the cannon which thunders its annual joyous return. When he invites any people willing to have slavery, to establish it, he is blowing out the moral lights around us" (*SW* 1:527; *CW* 3:29).[3] In truth, however, "the spirit of seventy-six and the spirit of Nebraska, are utter antagonisms" (*SW* 1:339; *CW* 2:275). Nebraskaism and Dred Scottism are a "burlesque upon judicial decisions, and [a] slander and profanation upon the honored names, and sacred history of republican America" (*SW* 1:418; *CW* 2:454).

3. Lincoln's imagery is taken from an 1827 speech by Henry Clay before the American Colonization Society, which he cites in his 1852 eulogy on Clay (*SW* 1:270; *CW* 2:131).

But how might a deluded people be made to see that? On the evidence of the Know-Nothings' popularity, Lincoln concludes, "Our progress in degeneracy appears to me to be pretty rapid" (*SW* 1:363; *CW* 2:323). If a profound change has in fact taken place, then the revolution is indeed incomplete. The union has not only to be saved; it must be so saved, so remade, as "to keep it, forever worthy of the saving." The soiled robe of republican America needs to be washed white "in the spirit, if not the blood, of the Revolution" (*SW* 1:339–40; *CW* 2:276). For Lincoln that can only mean a return to the Declaration of Independence.

(( ))

It belabors the obvious to recall that the Declaration is a great tocsin resounding throughout Lincoln's speeches and writings, evoking memory, alarm, and action. It is his point of departure and his point of return. There simply is no mistaking his regard for "the immortal paper" and its author (*SW* 1:702; *CW* 3:220). Lincoln's control and passion vie so impressively in this invocation that one may say that although the subject is hardly original with him, Lincoln emphatically makes it his own.

> All honor to Jefferson—to the man who, in the concrete pressure of a struggle for national independence by a single people, had the coolness, forecast, and capacity to introduce into a merely revolutionary document, an abstract truth, applicable to all men and all times, and so to embalm it there, that to-day, and in all coming days, it shall be a rebuke and a stumbling-block to the very harbingers of re-appearing tyrany and oppression (*SW* 2:19; *CW* 3:376).

He can in perfect truth declare, "I have never had a feeling politically that did not spring from the sentiments embodied in the Declaration of Independence" (*SW* 2:213; *CW* 4:240). Perhaps the most sublime achievement of Lincoln's *kalām* is the way he reshapes the debate raging over the extension of slavery in the western territories into a debate over the moral foundations of popular government. In that political world of antebellum America, so rife with political theologians and theological politicians, Lincoln succeeds in avoiding the excesses of each. He neither mistakes himself for the appointed agent of the Lord of Hosts nor falls into the idolatry of treating the voice of the majority as the voice of God. By insisting on making the Declaration of Independence the central point of reference, Lincoln is able to occupy a higher but still emphatically political ground. From that ground he can criticize the deniers, sappers, and traducers of its principles. From that high ground, too, he can identify and expose the unthinking forgetfulness that so conveniently encourages people to assume "there is no right principle of action but *self-interest*" (*SW* 1:315; *CW* 2:255). By pressing his case as a matter of high political principle—but a principle to which no white man can *afford* to assume or feign indifference—Lincoln leads a reluctant public to a disturbing confrontation with itself.

It is not enough to invoke, with pious tones, the right of self-government or the great principle of popular sovereignty. Where Douglas uses these formulas in an attempt to close off debate, Lincoln insists on using them to reconsider one's assumptions. "[I]f the negro *is* a man, is it not to that extent, a total destruction of self-government, to say that he too shall not govern *himself*? When the white man governs himself that is self-government; but when he governs himself, and also governs *another* man, that is *more* than self-government—that is despotism." No man, Lincoln insists, is good enough to govern another without that other's consent. That, if anything, is "the leading principle—the sheet anchor of American republicanism" (*SW* 1:328; *CW* 2:266). Again, the Declaration's assertion of human equality is not an assertion of equality in all respects but in some: in the right to life, liberty, and the pursuit of happiness, in "the right to put into his mouth the bread that his own hands have earned" (*SW*

1:477–78, 512; *CW* 2:520, 3:16). Denial of that principle will not and cannot stop with the black man. The argument that would justify enslaving a race is "the same old serpent" kings have used to bestride the necks of their people. In their fearful preoccupation with anything that might lift black men up, Douglas and those arguing like him are drawing white men down. They threaten to "destroy the principle that is the charter of our liberties" (*SW* 1:457; *CW* 2:500–501).

Lincoln takes special pains to so meld the principle and the charter that an attack on the one has to be an attack on the other. His enlarged interpretation of the Declaration's language and intention means that he can present Douglas's interpretation as a diminution, indeed a trivialization, of what even minimally is "the white man's charter of freedom" (*SW* 1:339; *CW* 2:276). In fact, Lincoln argues, the Declaration is much more. In its "noble words" lies the origin of popular sovereignty itself, or at least as applied to the Americans (*SW* 1:443–44, 583; *CW* 2:489, 3:94). And though it is indeed a charter of freedom, the Declaration embraces a much broader segment of humankind than only those people of British descent who were resident in North America in 1776. Slaves and Englishmen alike fall under its principles (*SW* 2:135; *CW* 4:16). Latecomers to America, European immigrants looking at its language, can "feel that that moral sentiment taught in that day evidences their relation to those men, that it is the father of all moral principle in them, and that they have a right to claim it as though they were blood of the blood, and flesh of the flesh of the men who wrote that Declaration, and so they are" (*SW* 1:456; *CW* 2:499–500). It is to the Declaration that Lincoln traces the genius of American independence. In it is to be found "the spirit which prizes liberty as the heritage of all men, in all lands, every where" (*SW* 1:585; *CW* 3:95).

The distinctiveness of America, even its special significance, lies in the stamp of the Declaration's principles upon the hearts and minds of people the world over. In this connection Lincoln has the boldness to speak not simply of his regard for "the opinions and examples of our revolutionary fathers" and of his love for "the sentiments of those old-time men" (*SW* 1:329; *CW* 2:267). From Independence Hall's "consecrated," "holy and most sacred walls" one may still hear "breathings rising"; "the teachings coming forth from that sacred hall" are less an episode of the past than a continuing presence. On the eve of his most dreadful new responsibilities, it is to these teachings that Lincoln sees fit to pledge his devotion. In so doing he uses terms that echo the Psalmist's devotion to Jerusalem as he sat weeping by the waters of Babylon (*SW* 2:212; *CW* 4:239). It was no mere wordsmith's trope that led him to speak years earlier of "my ancient faith" and of "our ancient faith" (*SW* 1:328; *CW* 2:266), and to warn of "giving up the OLD for the NEW faith" (*SW* 1:339; *CW* 2:275). But in rendering the ancestral sacred, Lincoln takes care, as we shall see, to keep it within human reach as an object of warm familiarity. It is "that old Declaration of Independence" and the sentiments of "those old men" (*SW* 1:443, 456–57; *CW* 2:488, 499), "the good old one, penned by Jefferson" (*SW* 2:259; *CW* 4:438), that he keeps before the public eye. To lose these would be to lose the better part of one's self.

Thus the brunt of Lincoln's charge against Douglas's reading of the Declaration is not quite what one might have expected. By maintaining that the black man is not included in its language, Douglas is tending "to take away from him the right of ever striving to be a man" (*SW* 1:798; *CW* 3:304); that is bad enough. But this evil is exceeded by the long-term effect of such thinking: "penetrating the human soul and eradicating the light of reason and the love of liberty in this American people," "he is blowing out the moral lights around us" (*SW* 1:527, 717; *CW* 3:29, 234).[4] This loss is not conjectural but actual. "When we were the political slaves of King George, and wanted to be free, we called the maxim that 'all men are created equal' a self evident truth; but now when

4. Ibid.

we have grown fat, and have lost all dread of being slaves ourselves, we have become so greedy to be *masters* that we call the same maxim 'a self-evident lie'" (*SW* 1:359; *CW* 2:318). What once had been "held sacred by all, and thought to include all" now is "assailed, and sneered at, and construed, and hawked at, and torn" beyond recognition (*SW* 1:396; *CW* 2:404). In calling for a readoption of the Declaration and a return to the practices and policy that harmonized with it, Lincoln is also calling for America to return to its promise.

Lincoln never argues that the fulfillment of that promise is easy or at hand. Yet the overall effect of the Declaration's principle gives cause for hope and for pride: "its constant working has been a steady progress towards the practical equality of all men" (*SW* 1:386; *CW* 2:385). In what still remains the outstanding characterization of the Declaration, Lincoln speaks of its authors meaning to set up "a standard maxim for free society, which should be familiar to all, and revered by all; constantly looked to, constantly labored for, and even though never perfectly attained, constantly approximated, and thereby constantly spreading and deepening its influence, and augmenting the happiness and value of life to all people of all colors everywhere" (*SW* 1:398; *CW* 2:406).[5] Shorn of its universal intent, of what practical use can that old declaration be? "Mere rubbish—old wadding left to rot on the battle-field" (*SW* 1:400; *CW* 2:407). The grandeur of America is inseparable from its founders' dreams. In daring to give "hope to the world for all future time" (*SW* 2:213; *CW* 4:240), they secured an immortal fame for themselves and their successors.

5. Lincoln uses comparable language in describing the effects of "the just and generous, and prosperous system" of free labor (*SW* 2:98, 297; *CW* 3:479, 5:52).

(( ))

Since Lincoln fixes his eye so firmly on the moral aspect of the American Revolution, he attends as a matter of course to the characters of those who made it. Not surprisingly, he finds those men admirable, although not simply so. Though Lincoln is often eager to present them as figures on a pedestal, he is also able to place them in a somewhat less flattering light. The main thrust of his remarks, however, is to present them as benefactors. Lincoln rings many changes on that theme. He, his contemporaries, and Americans yet unborn all owe gratitude to that race of ancestors, those "iron men" who bequeathed them such fundamental blessings (*SW* 1:28, 455; *CW* 1:108, 2:499). Beyond that, the patriots of '76 are models and objects of emulation. Just as they pledged their lives, their fortunes, and their sacred honor in support of the Declaration of Independence, their successors ought to pledge their all in support of the Constitution and the laws (*SW* 1:32; *CW* 1:112). Lincoln even goes so far as to urge that his contemporaries adopt the salutary habit of regarding the Constitution as unalterable. "The men who made it, have done their work, and have passed away. Who shall improve, on what *they* did?" (*SW* 1:196; *CW* 1:488).

Yet moving in tandem with this vein of filiopiety is a subdued but unmistakable demythologizing. Lincoln's founders are indeed great men—but men, not demigods. Those who ran the risk of failure, derision, and oblivion in order to make the revolution only dared what any might do who "naturally seek the gratification of their ruling passion." Staking "their *all*" upon their success, those men of ambition wagered—and won celebrity, fame, and distinction (*SW* 1:34; *CW* 1:113). Whatever the broader reach of their benefaction, its motivating impulse could not be called selfless.

Nonetheless, models they were and models they remain for Lincoln. He does not cease urging his fellows, "degenerated men (if we have degenerated)," to follow the opinions and examples of "those noble fathers—Washington, Jefferson and Madison" (*SW* 2:76; *CW* 3:453). It is obvious that this insistent message is not meant to be taken as a commendation of mindless adulation; for beyond the level of prattling babes, Lincoln has not a single good word to say in favor of mindlessness of any sort.

Now and here, let me guard a little against being misunderstood. I do not mean to say we are bound to follow implicitly in whatever our fathers did. To do so, would be to discard all the lights of current experience—to reject all progress—all improvement. What I do say is, that if we would supplant the opinions and policy of our fathers in any case, we should do so upon evidence so conclusive, and argument so clear, that even their great authority, fairly considered and weighed, cannot stand; and most surely not in a case whereof we ourselves declare they understood the question better than we (*SW* 2:119; *CW* 3:534–35).

In nothing, perhaps, are the fathers more to be followed, more to be studied, more to be imitated, than in their opposition to slavery. Here especially, according to Lincoln, they showed their moral clarity and their political prudence. They knew "a vast moral evil" when they saw it (*SW* 1:450; *CW* 2:494). When and as they could, they put "the seal of legislation *against its spread*" (*SW* 1:514; *CW* 3:18). They assiduously eschewed and rejected anything suggesting that one might have a moral right to enslave another. "The argument of 'Necessity' was the only argument they ever admitted in favor of slavery; and so far, and so far only as it carried them, did they ever go" (*SW* 1:337, 478, 765, 802; *CW* 2:274, 520, 3:276, 308). They intended, expected, and encouraged the public to expect, that slavery ultimately would become extinct (*SW* 1:448, 603, 800, 2:70–71; *CW* 2:492, 3:117, 306, 448). This, according to Lincoln, was the position of the leading men of the revolution and the position to which they "stuck . . . through thick and thin." "Through their whole course, from first to last, they clung to freedom" (*SW* 2:48; *CW* 3:416).

Purer souls, sterner moralists, can and do argue that, far from being models for emulation, the architects of American constitutionalism were temporizers, or whistlers in the dark, or even covenanters with Satan himself. Where such critics may see weakness and confusion, Lincoln unhesitatingly perceives prudence. The premise of his admiration is plain enough: "From the necessities of the case we should be compelled to form just such a government as our blessed fathers gave us" (SW 2:136–37; CW 4:18). Again, what Lincoln has in mind is a defense not of every jot and tittle of earlier policies and provisions but of the general stance the founders took toward the actual presence of slavery in the new nation. Its presence was a fact, no less a fact than its being a wrong. Neither fact might be ignored or wished away, and the authors of the Declaration responded to both. At one and the same time they both declared the right of all to the equal enjoyment of inalienable rights and took account of the circumstances standing in the way of an immediate universal attainment of these rights (SW 1:398; CW 2:406). A moral imperative was embedded in a far-from-yielding world and then left to work its influence. In surrounding the existing evil with constitutional guards, the forefathers bought peace. But in doing so they did not compromise their understanding of the evil as an evil (SW 1:581–82; CW 3:92–93). "You may have a wen or a cancer upon your person and not be able to cut it out lest you bleed to death; but surely it is no way to cure it, to engraft it and spread it over your whole body." "The peaceful way, the old-fashioned way" of the fathers is the model for others to follow as well (SW 1:808, 2:38; CW 3:313, 407).

The cancer metaphor also appears in another discussion of the founders' prudence. Lincoln is struck, as others must be, by the "ambiguous, roundabout, and mystical" language used in the Constitution's provisions respecting slavery (SW 2:142; CW 4:22). "That covert language," he says, "was used with a purpose" and with an eye to the time when, slavery having expired among the Americans, "there should be nothing on the face of the great charter of liberty suggesting that such a thing as negro slavery had ever existed among us" (*SW* 1:801–2; *CW* 3:307). Without quite saying so, Lincoln implies that the circumlocution was prompted by a sense of shame.

> Thus, the thing is hid away, in the constitution, just as an afflicted man hides away a wen or a cancer, which he dares not cut out at once, lest he bleed to death; with the promise, nevertheless, that the cutting may begin at the end of a given time. Less than this our fathers COULD not do; and MORE they WOULD not do. Necessity drove them so far, and farther, they would not go (*SW* 1:338; *CW* 2:274).

Principle had made its painful peace with circumstance.

It is to this policy, at once moral and prudential, that Lincoln urges his countrymen to return. In a tireless succession of speeches stretching from 1854 to 1860, he makes the point again and again: by returning to the policy of the fathers, by returning slavery to the position they originally marked out for it, by insisting on treating slavery as an evil (albeit one with constitutional protections), and by restoring the legitimate public expectation that slavery should ultimately become extinct, the country will regain peace and national self-respect (*SW* 1:340, 458, 470, 514, 803; *CW* 2:276, 501, 513, 3:18, 308). In this sense it is Douglas himself, not Lincoln and those whom Douglas calls Black Republicans, who is the radical innovator. It is Douglas who cannot let slavery "stand upon the basis upon which our fathers placed it, but removed it and *put it upon the cotton gin basis*" (*SW* 1:766, 811–12; *CW* 3:276, 316).

Against the charge that the Republicans are revolutionary and destructive, Lincoln insists upon the ancestral credentials of the new party's program. In seeking to "restore this government to its original tone" as regards slavery, the party's chief and real purpose is "eminently conservative" (*SW* 2:35, 147; *CW* 3:404, 4:27). Douglas's version of American history cannot—and, under Lincoln's relentless pressure, will not—

conceal the gap between the principles of the contemporary Democratic party and those of its slaveowner-founder, who had confessed that "he trembled for his country when he remembered that God was just" (*SW* 1:702; *CW* 3:220). As between the "don't care" policy of the one and the anguished contemplation of the other, Lincoln urges his fellows: "Choose ye between Jefferson and Douglas as to what is the true view of this element among us" (*SW* 2:42; *CW* 3:410).

Lincoln's recurrence to the history of the sentiments, policies, and actions of the founders is both a tactical move and a profound necessity. It is both a recollection and a reconception. He believes that his is by far the stronger case, although some later students doubt whether the evidentiary record is as unequivocal as he makes it out to be.[6] Ultimately, Lincoln's historical narrative is a moral tale whose fervor and un-

---

6. The most diverse interpreters assert or concede as much before going on to draw utterly incompatible conclusions. Thus, for example, Harry V. Jaffa (in a seminal study to which I am much in debt) allows that "Lincoln's affirmation of the Founders' and signers' meaning, as distinct from his contradiction of Douglas and Taney, is not itself impeccable on purely historical grounds" and surmises that Lincoln "was not innocent of the nature of his subsequent 'reconstruction'" of their meaning. Jaffa, *Crisis of the House Divided: An Interpretation of the Issues in the Lincoln-Douglas Debates* (New York: Doubleday, 1959), 328 (see also 324, 325). M. E. Bradford charges Lincoln with being "duplicitous" while "appealing to an imaginary history." Bradford, "Against Lincoln," in *The Historian's Lincoln: Pseudohistory, Psychohistory, and History*, edited by Gabor S. Boritt and Norman O. Forness (Urbana: University of Illinois Press, 1988), 111. Garry Wills sees Lincoln's self-conscious artistry as contributing to a romantic, mythic misreading—if not distortion— of Jefferson's principles and intentions. Wills, *Inventing America: Jefferson's Declaration of Independence* (New York: Vintage Books, 1979), xiv–xxiv. More charitable, perhaps, is the assertion by Mark E. Neely, Jr., that "the Jeffersonian legacy was more ambiguous than Lincoln realized." Neely, *The Abraham Lincoln Encyclopedia*, s.v. "Jefferson, Thomas" (New York: McGraw-Hill, 1982), 164.

mistakable force derive from the centrality he accords the Declaration of Independence. He understands with unrivaled clarity that the Declaration's principle of "Liberty to all" has to be "*the* word, '*fitly spoken*' which has proved an 'apple of gold' to us."[7] The union and the character of the union depend upon the sense that each American has of being historically connected with the nation's astonishing rise to prosperity and might. The recollection of the beginnings, as on the annual Fourth of July celebrations, is a reminder that the bonds are not primarily genetic but moral. The Declaration's principle is "the father of all moral principle" in the founders' descendants, adoptive as well as biological. But if public sentiment were knowingly or unknowingly corrupted, that principle could no longer serve as "the electric cord" linking together "the hearts of patriotic and liberty-loving men" (*SW* 1:456; *CW* 2:499–500). Lincoln's appeals not to break these bonds of affection came too late. In the land of the deaf, the forgetful, and the shrill, the mystic chords of memory would be silenced by guns at Charleston Harbor.

7. See Lincoln's meditation on Proverbs 25:11 in *CW*, 4:168–69.

7

Tocqueville's Political Sermon

The more impressive a work of historical analysis, the greater the likelihood it will deceive. Whether a popular article or a scholarly monograph, its aura of completeness and balance, even its physical unity, may serve to conceal the field of diverse forces at whose intersections the historian stands. Like the coroner's report or the chemist's analysis, the historian's handiwork is a function of the interplay of investigating mind and subject matter. Beyond that, however, it also involves the reciprocal shaping of author and audience; for as with a playwright or a politician, the historian's effort to persuade or to alter conventional outlooks is limited by what the audience will bear. Last, and usually least visible to readers of histories, are authors' efforts to maintain some critical distance from their contemporaries. The attempt to see some earlier age for what it was obliges an author first to see the current age for what it is. For to the extent that the historian's stance toward peoples of the past rests upon the unexamined premises of the present, his work is apt to mistake present prejudices for past certainties. Wishing simultaneously to locate himself *in* a time while rising *above* it, the historian repeatedly soars and sinks, until at last, like an erratic kite, he settles to the ground—his own ground.

This bracing tension between inquirer and milieu is almost palpable in Alexis de Tocqueville's two great works, *Democracy in America* and *The Old Regime and the Revolution*. In each, Tocqueville seeks not so much to see differently than his contemporaries as to see farther and higher. In each, he has to contend with well-entrenched opinions whose practical effects he judges to be exacerbating the dangers and sickness of his age. And in each, he seeks a means of prodding the complacent to take heed and of helping the fearful to take heart.

Yet any hopes Tocqueville might entertain of affecting the new democratic order lie under a dark misgiving that the social analyst too may be dominated by the presumptions and structures of the current age. Like their contemporaries, historians take their initial bearings by what lies closest to hand and appears most usual. Unless they are exceptionally alert and wary, they will slip into prevailing modes of explanation and expression. If they live in an age when singular figures are held to make all the difference, they too are apt to focus their attention on such individuals and forget the rest. Similarly, historians who live in an age when individuals seem to matter hardly at all are likely in their analyses to resort to "very general causes" rather than to causes of a "secondary and accidental nature." This is more than a matter of subjective belief or of being taken in by surface appearances. General causes do indeed explain more, and particular influences less, in democratic than in aristocratic ages. And in fact the opposite is true in aristocratic times: the inequality of conditions prevailing then makes it possible for a few leading actors "to go against the natural inclinations of all the rest." In mimicking and thereby exaggerating those features of their respective ages, both aristocratic and democratic historians reinforce prevailing patterns of thought and action. Consequently, the effects of their teachings may be misleading, even pernicious. Indeed, it is striking that Tocqueville appears less concerned with the truth or falsity of these alternative modes of historical explanation than with their social consequences: "Classical historians taught how to command; those of our own time teach next to nothing but how to obey. In their writings the author often figures large, but humanity is always tiny."[1]

Precisely because Tocqueville sees in all this much more than an arid academic exercise, he is prone to view the writers of histories (himself included) as political actors. In democratic ages, he implies, the typical run of historians may be likened to carriers of an infectious disease. Their readiness to invoke great impersonal forces conveys an unmistakable lesson to their democratic readers: namely, that there is no point in resisting causes so vast and universal. "For my part," Tocqueville reiterates in his *Recollections*, "I hate all those absolute systems that make all the events of history depend on great first causes linked together by the chain of fate and [which] thus succeed, so to speak, in banishing men from the history of the human race. Their boasted breadth seems to me narrow, and their mathematical exactness false."[2]

Thus the restoration of secondary causes or accidental circumstances to their rightful importance is tantamount to giving the particular wills of individuals their due. By reinstating the individual as a significant actor in the account of things past, it becomes possible to make a place for human excellence in the shape of things to come. This ulterior

1. Alexis de Tocqueville, *Democracy in America*, trans. George Lawrence (New York: Harper & Row, 1966), 462–65 (vol. 2, pt. 1, chap. 20). For Tocqueville's confessed lapse into prevalent (and misleading) locutions, see ibid., 450 (vol. 2, pt. 1, chap. 16).

2. Alexis de Tocqueville, *Recollections*, trans. George Lawrence (Garden City, N.Y.: Doubleday, 1970), 62 (pt. 2, chap. 1).

political motive stands in the forefront of Tocqueville's concerns as he engages in his historical researches. While he disavows any intention to prescribe a remedy for the condition into which the Old Regime, the Republic, and the Empire successively plunged France, it by no means follows that his work in progress, *The Old Regime and the Revolution*, would leave the reader "uncertain as to the judgments he should adopt. . . . It would be very odd if—bringing to this study tastes so decided and often so impassioned, ideas so set, a goal to reach for that is so visible to me and so fixed—I left the reader without any impetus whatsoever, wandering at random in the midst of my thoughts and of his." But rather than tell readers dogmatically (and ineffectively) what they ought to think, it makes more sense to Tocqueville to "set their minds on the road leading to truths" and compel them to find these for themselves. Thus Tocqueville's history would exemplify precisely the kind of historical writing that democrats and the democratic age stand most in need of and are least likely to get.

> . . . I am quite convinced that political societies are not what their laws make them, but what sentiments, beliefs, ideas, habits of the heart, and the spirit of the men who form them, prepare them in advance to be, as well as what nature and education have made them. If this truth does not emerge, at every turn, from my book, if it does not induce the readers to reflect, in this way, unceasingly on themselves, if it does not indicate at every instant, without ever having the pretense of instructing them, what are the sentiments, the ideas, the mores that alone can lead to public prosperity and liberty, what are the vices and errors that, on the other hand, divert them irresistibly from this, I will not have attained the principal and, as it were, unique goal that I have in view.[3]

3. Tocqueville to Claude-François de Corcelle, 17 Sept. 1853, in Alexis de Tocqueville, *Selected Letters on Politics and Society*, edited

The intentions here voiced are the themes of a lifetime. As a young adult Tocqueville is already persuaded that "each man should account to society for his thoughts, as well as for his physical energy. When one sees one's fellows in danger, one's duty is to go to their aid."[4] Out of this belief arises his decision to write about democracy in America. Similarly, Tocqueville's perception that "the natural vices of the race unfortunately coincide with the natural vices of the [democratic] social state" gives special urgency to his sense of duty. People in such a society slide all too easily into habits of mediocrity and pettiness. They are more than ready to believe that they live in a smaller and meaner place than where their forebears had situated their nation. To entertain such beliefs is "not healthy." A people ought not to be permitted to console itself for its decline "by making railroads"; a sense of humiliation is too high a price to pay for individual prosperity.[5]

Tocqueville's convictions are reinforced by the contrast he sees between the exaggerated confidence—"a noble error"—of the previous century and the equally excessive humility of the present. It is worth considering how one ought to address a people suffering from "the great malady of the time." Surely

---

by Roger Boesche, trans. James Toupin and Roger Boesche (Berkeley: University of California Press, 1985), 293–94. The restraint avowed here calls to mind the exemplary method of another "politic historiographer": "Digressions for instruction's cause, and other such open conveyances of precepts, (which is the philosopher's part), he never useth; as having so clearly set before men's eyes the ways and events of good and evil counsels, that the narration itself doth secretly instruct the reader, and more effectually than can possibly be done by precept." Thomas Hobbes, "To the Readers" and "Of the Life and History of Thucydides," in *Hobbes's Thucydides*, edited by Richard Schlatter (New Brunswick, N.J.: Rutgers University Press, 1975), 7, 18.

4. Tocqueville to Louis de Kergorlay, Jan. 1835, *Selected Letters*, 95.

5. Tocqueville to John Stuart Mill, 18 Mar. 1841, *Selected Letters*, 150–51.

not by confirming their sense of helplessness and hopeless-
ness.[6] Rather, "one must not despise man, if one wants to
obtain great efforts from others and from oneself." "I want to
treat them as men, in effect."[7] It is in this respect that Tocqueville's masterpiece of his maturity, *The Old Regime and the
Revolution*, might be regarded as his political sermon of 1856.
His blasted hopes of 1848 and 1849, so vividly detailed in his
secret memoirs, hardly resonate here. Although ailing and
despondent, the revolutionary historian would make one last
great effort and bring forth not a confession of defeat but a
call to energetic striving.

(())

Two figures loom above all others in *The Old Regime and
the Revolution*: the French nation and the author. It is not
surprising that the French should be so prominent in this
work, for its subject, announced at the outset, is the unprece-
dented effort of that people "to separate by an abyss that
which they had hitherto been from that which they wished
henceforth to be" (Preface, 69).[8] It is certainly less obvious,
perhaps less fitting, maybe even unseemly, that Tocqueville
should be the other great presence visible in this work. His

6. Tocqueville to Arthur de Gobineau, 20 Dec. 1853, *Selected
Letters*, 303. Predestination, whether prompted by a materialist
philosophy or a spiritualist theology, can be "pernicious," "su-
premely immoral." Tocqueville to Gobineau, 17 Nov. 1853, *Selected
Letters*, 297–300; Tocqueville to Kergorlay, 4 Aug. 1857, *Selected
Letters*, 357.

7. Tocqueville to Gustave de Beaumont, 22 Apr. 1838, *Selected
Letters*, 130; Tocqueville to Gobineau, 24 Jan. 1857, *Selected Letters*,
347.

8. Parenthetical references are to the book and chapter of the text.
The number following the comma indicates the page in the French
edition: Alexis de Tocqueville, *Oeuvres complètes*, edited by J.-P.
Mayer, 13 vols. in 22 pts. to date, vol. 2, pt. 1, *L'Ancien Régime et la
Révolution* (Paris: Gallimard, 1952).

placing himself between us and his subject, although hardly as pronounced as in the case of Michelet, nonetheless startles us as readers of histories. It is enough to make us wonder whether Tocqueville's work even belongs to that genre. In fact, his opening sentence disavows that characterization, asserting rather that the book is "a study on that Revolution" (Preface, 69). Yet no matter how we classify the work, we still must wonder what legitimate authorial purpose is served by his having us see so much of him in this book. In pursuit of the answer to this question, we shall look again at the preface.

Like Taine's preface to his *Ancient Regime*, and indeed like prefaces to many other books, Tocqueville's is an occasion to tell something of how he came to his study, what he means to bring to light in it, and where future researches should go. Tocqueville's study originates in a doubt, his doubt that the French revolutionaries understood what they were about. But to second-guess them he must first disinter a France that is no more. That operation turns out to be much harder than he had suspected, and he is compelled to study the eighteenth century with a thoroughness unmatched by any prior investigator. The spectacle he portrays of an aristocrat rummaging through musty archives, far from being ludicrous, is meant to impress. His efforts have been tireless, his appetite for materials apparently boundless. Famous books and justly obscure ones, public documents and unpublished manuscripts, even the vast archival riches of confidential communications under the Old Regime—all are handled, scrutinized, and weighed. From his privileged position Tocqueville is able to know much that contemporaries could not know, "for I had beneath my eyes that which they were never permitted to see" (Preface, 71).

The offhand way in which Tocqueville speaks of his coming to live on such familiar terms with the Frenchmen of the Old Regime (Preface, 72), the repeated references to his great efforts ("Quite a short chapter has sometimes cost me more than one year's research" [Preface, 76]), to his infinite pains (ii:1, 100), and to his patience (ii:1, 102), all lend special weight and significance to his reported agitations of soul. The more impressed we are with his credentials as a careful investigator, the more likely we are to sit up and take note of his astonishment (Preface, 71; i:4, 91; ii:11, 171; iii:1, 201), his wonder (i:4, 92), and his surprise (ii:3, 119; ii:12, 188). If Tocqueville, on going through the "immense work" of examining and assembling all the many demands of the *cahiers* of the three estates, is taken over by "a sort of terror" (iii:1, 197), if he is "almost startled" by his discoveries (ii:12, 188), then we too should share his perturbations. We participate in the education he receives while studying the Old Regime.

Tocqueville's persistence in keeping himself before the reader might be seen then as part of a larger effort—that of establishing credit with the reader. It is not, after all, enough to be told that "we are placed today at that precise point from which this great subject can best be perceived and judged" (i:1, 82). If we are to accept such a portentous judgment, we need to see the credentials of the observer making it. If *The Old Regime and the Revolution* were a mere history, it would be enough to believe that the historian is assiduous (Preface, 69–70), without prejudice or fear of offending (Preface, 73), and open to the force of new evidence (ii:11, 173; iii:3, 217). That Tocqueville does not leave it at that suggests the possibility that he cannot leave it at that, which in turn reinforces the suspicion that one is dealing with something more than a history.

Two features of Tocqueville's address in particular call for comment. One is his frequent recurrence to conversational tone, even direct address, in the course of presenting his findings. For example: "Bear this in mind," he tells you (i:4, 94); "Picture to yourself, I ask you, the French peasant of the eighteenth century, or rather the peasant you know, for he is always the same" (ii:1, 106); "Come now and see what becomes of a deserted class" (ii:12, 181); "You would think this book was written yesterday: it is one hundred years old" (iii:3, 214); "Read the minutes . . . , study the other public documents . . . , [and] you will be touched . . . and surprised" (iii:5, 229). In reporting his findings Tocqueville relives before our eyes his activities and feelings as a historical researcher, sometimes speaking to us over his shoulder with the papers spread before him, sometimes speaking to us face to face, as it were, and in the present tense (see, for example, ii:1, 100–101; ii:12, 185; iii:1, 197; iii:3, 214). Author and reader are on such terms that the author can even use sarcasm without risk of being out of place or mistaken (see, for example, ii:3, 119; ii:4, 125; ii:6, 131 and 132; ii:9, 155; ii:10, 166; iii:1, 200; and note to ii:11, 294).

The other feature of Tocqueville's address that bears comment is his singular manner of insinuating the weight of his evidence and the authority with which it invests his argument. Most often we are assured that what is being shown is only the tip of the iceberg, "one example out of a thousand"; the sheer mass of evidence awaits us if only we would follow Tocqueville down into M. de Grandmaison's archives (e.g., ii:3, 122; ii:6, 137; ii:7, 140; ii:9, 149; and notes to ii:1, 273; ii:2, 276; ii:3, 284; ii:5, 287; ii:11, 293). But such herculean efforts on our part are dispensable. We can retrace Tocqueville's steps a little way, confirm his finding, and be satisfied (e.g., ii:2, 109). Or, easier still, we can rest assured that he has held the documents in his own hands (e.g., ii:12, 184; iii:5, 230; and note to ii:1, 272). (We have not yet entered the age when the reader's faith rests on the author's faith in his research assistant.) All evidence in this book, we come to feel, is exemplary; one case is as good as a thousand because brooding behind the one are the thousand. By the same token, the telling example's force draws on our waxing assurance that Tocqueville's example is not idiosyncratic or atypical; it grips us and it reveals *because* it is typical. For example, take the spectacle of the highest nobility of the land begging off the payment of their tax, addressing the local Intendant (a man of humble birth, a young man on the make), as "Monseigneur" (ii:6, 137; and note to ii:10, 291–92). The persuasive power of such examples depends upon our sense that these are distillates, rare essences extracted from a mass of matter.

Tocqueville confesses, but without apology, that he has written this book with passion. As with any Frenchman, he says, feeling pervades his speech about his country, his thought about his times (Preface, 73). Could it be otherwise? But unlike most Frenchmen, Tocqueville works that feeling into an elaborate design, a construct that enables his book to serve simultaneously as an analysis of the past, a tract for the times, and a reflection on the future. His enlistment of our feeling may be indispensable for each of these different aspects of the work. In any event, this is clearly a book in which a Frenchman addresses his compatriots. With very few exceptions, "we" or "us" or "our" refers to the French (but see iii:2, 208; iii:7, 238). Postrevolutionary Frenchmen are occasionally distinguished from the earlier generations, but most often the talk is of an enduring people to whom, for all their differences and divisions, one can still speak of "our history" (ii:9, 150; iii:1, 201; iii:3, 210), "our nation" (iii:8, 249), "our nature" (iii:1, 200; see also iii:8, 249), and "our race" (iii:1, 200). Given all the talk of "our fathers" (Preface, 73; ii:1, 105; ii:10, 164; ii:11, 176; iii:1, 197), even of "our fathers of 1789" (iii:3, 216), we are prepared for talk not only of "the Revolution" but of "our Revolution" (i:1, 79; iii:2, 207; iii:3, 216), even of "our anti-religious philosophy" (iii:2, 206).

These constant reminders of the bonds between author and audience are neither mindless nor gratuitous. The subject of Tocqueville's book is, after all, highly charged with politics. He is himself a political man whose views on matters of contention have been made public in print and in speech over a period of two decades. And yet far from glossing over the positions that set him at odds with his fellows, Tocqueville pointedly reminds the reader of his now unseasonable remarks of twenty years ago (Preface, 73–75). This may seem a curious way to shake off the reproach of being old-fashioned, yet for Tocqueville's purposes it makes good sense. However important it may be that the reader feel a bond of solidarity with the author, the realization of Tocqueville's purposes requires no less that the reader—without blinking—also see the gulf between them. Tocqueville's book does not promise us more of what we already believe; still less does it offer comforting thoughts. Author, reader, and argument remain poised between the mutual confidence of familiars and the tension that attends the discovery of startling and possibly unpleasant truths.

(( ))

Although (if I am not mistaken) Tocqueville does not himself use the word "method" to characterize his mode of inquiry in this book, he invites the reader's attention to his method. He compares his way of asking, looking, and reporting to the ways of an anatomist (or a pathologist) and to the ways of a painter. In studying the old, Tocqueville does not lose sight of the new; in dissecting a corpse, he looks to discover both the cause of death and the means by which death might have been averted. "I have acted like those doctors, who in each lifeless organ attempt to surprise the laws of life" (Preface, 73). Because France is no vile body, and because Tocqueville is a Frenchman, indifference parading as detachment would be entirely inappropriate. The microscopic examination of deformities (note to ii:5, 286) is not to be conducted as it might be during a study of *Drosophila*.

It would be not so much wrong as dull to drop Tocqueville's book into the bin labeled "didactic history." Edifying accounts evoke memories which in themselves can induce yawning among healthy people. Yet nothing could be farther from the experience of readers of this book. Still, it is undeniable that Tocqueville's book belongs not only to that large class of histories that have something to tell but also to that smaller class of works that have something to teach. Further, by his own admission Tocqueville stands guilty of didactic intent (Preface, 73).

My aim has been to draw a picture strictly accurate and at the same time instructive. Every time then that I have met among our fathers any of those masculine virtues, which are most necessary to us and yet are almost extinct—a true spirit of independence, the taste for great things, faith in ourselves and in a cause—I have set them in relief, and correspondingly, when in the laws, in the ideas, in the manners of that bygone age, I have met with any trace of some of the vices which, after having destroyed ancient society, still afflict us, I have taken care to put them in the limelight, in order that, seeing well the evil they have already done, we might better understand what further evil they might do us.

The political lessons abounding in this work—stated as they are with subtlety, complexity, and a beauty that survives even translation—deserve something better than flat summary. The pleasure of discovery, which Tocqueville's art strives so to recreate in the reader's soul, should remain intact for the reader, unsullied by a commentator's good intentions. One theme, however, may be selected for closer examination, not because it is proof against botching, but because it is central to our concern with the peculiar rhetorical and stylistic features of Tocqueville's *kalām*.

Tocqueville studies the effort of the revolutionary French to deny themselves, to cut themselves off utterly from their past, to begin anew in every conceivable way. The how and the why of the failure of this staggering enterprise is the subject of that larger but uncompleted whole of which *The Old Regime and the Revolution* is a part. And yet, notwithstanding their failure to radically alter their character, the fact remains that the French of '89 resemble the French of the Second Empire about as much as the Spartans of Thermopylae resemble the Social Security pensioners now resident in the villages of Laconia. Far from muting those differences, Tocqueville sets them in relief. We seem, then, to be left with two highly unsatisfactory conclusions. The actions of the men of '89, who treated national character as though it were nought, were acts of truly heroic folly; the actions of the men of '89 display a great-spiritedness and audacity and unselfishness that we hardly can recognize in any Frenchman we know. For Tocqueville to accomplish his larger political purpose in writing this book he must bring these two conclusions into some intelligible relation.

Now there is no doubt that Tocqueville's argument presupposes that there is such a thing as national character. Indeed, this book might as justly be called a study on national character as a study on the French Revolution. The French, according to Tocqueville, exhibit fixity and flux to a higher degree than any other nation: France is home to "a people so unalterable in its primary instincts that it is recognizable in its portraits drawn two or three thousand years ago, and at the same time so changeable in its daily thoughts and in its tastes that it ends by becoming a spectacle surprising to itself" (iii:8, 249). Discerning what is permanent is no simple task; one can easily mistake the results of a "singular education" for what some people have called "*the French spirit*" (iii:1, 200–201). Yet discerning what is permanent, and discriminating between it and the results of a defective or deforming education, are among the first steps to be taken by any would-be reformer of a people's social and political life.

Thus while the men and events of '89 are a foil for Tocqueville's withering attack on the French of his time, they are no less an intimation of what this people might yet become. In this respect Tocqueville's repeated praises of the men of '89 are not simply to be canceled out by his repeated condemnations of those very men; the moral bookkeeping does not run that way. Rather, the virtues of the revolutionaries are to be compared with the virtues of their descendants, the vices of the men of '89 with the vices of the French people nine or ten "perpetual" constitutions later. The contrast invites despair. (See, for example, Preface, 72; i:1, 79; i:2, 83; ii:11, 175–77; iii:2, 207–8; iii:3, 214; iii:8, 247–48.)

Yet Tocqueville does not give in to despair. He attempts instead to locate the sources of those differences, concluding that the present-day diminution of the French is owing not to the failure of the revolution but to its success. In much the same way, the bravura plans and acts of the men of '89 derive not from the success of the Old Regime but from its failure. Both those who conducted the affairs of the Old Regime and those who after the first heady moments came to conduct the affairs of the New Order tirelessly pursued policies that isolated individuals and classes from one another, sought in countless ways to rid Frenchmen of those occasions when they might experience the pains and joys of self-governance, and acted almost uniformly on the assumption that the people of all classes were fit only for tutelage.

Although the old France could still bring forth "those vigorous souls, those proud and daring spirits . . . which were to make the French Revolution at once the admiration and the terror of the generations that followed it" (ii:11, 177), this fecundity was the other side of outworn and embarrassing institutions and habits of mind. Paradoxically, many of the very injustices and absurdities most opposed to the establishment of a regular and beneficent freedom were themselves the source of a peculiar form of greatness. Thus the intransigent haughtiness of the eighteenth-century nobility—hollow, self-serving, and ridiculous though it was—predisposed those nobles to run risks, to oppose both enslavement and the rule of law. Their pride of heart not only led to displays of "the manly virtues" but served to encourage "the manliness of the other classes" (ii:11, 169–70). The middle class, too, hot in pursuit of the immunities and privileges that would make them into a pseudoaristocracy, were drawn into a public defense of their corporate, self-seeking concerns. The truckling coward among them could not hide himself in a crowd (ii:11, 173). With the vast exception of the common people, no eighteenth-century Frenchman was without his place in a society where he could be seen and make himself heard, where (if he had the courage) he could "bicker over his obedience and resist even while yielding." Loving joy and adoring pleasure, the French were not yet hostages to "that judicious and well-regulated sensualism that we see [around us]"; they still could dare (ii:11, 175–76).

The men of the eighteenth century hardly knew that kind of passion for material comfort which is the mother of servitude, an enervating but tenacious and unalterable passion, which readily mingles with and, so to speak, twines itself round many private virtues such as love of family, respectability of life, regard for religious beliefs, and even the assiduous if lukewarm practice of the established worship, which is partial to respectability but forbids heroism, which excels in making men steady but citizens mean-spirited.

Thus the pitiably meager opportunities for an education in freedom afforded by the Old Regime were nonetheless enough to produce the generous enthusiasts of '89, those disbelievers who at least still retained "one admirable belief that we lack": belief in themselves (iii:2, 207). The result of their labors is a world without their likes, the world of Tocqueville's readers.

The new France, having succeeded in ridding itself of almost every last trace of what so offends administrators and Economists, now enjoys the fruits of its triumph. If it once was possible to see men of the caliber of '89, that was because "the art of stifling the sound of all resistance had not then been brought to the perfection that it has reached today. France had not yet become the deafened place in which we live" (ii:11, 173). To see in such words any praise or defense or endorsement of the Old Regime would be odd, especially in the light of Tocqueville's repeated condemnations of that order. (See, for example, ii:3, 116; ii:6, 132, 134; ii:9, 154–55; ii:10, 166; and note to ii:9, 289.) Certainly this book issues no call for a return or restoration of the Old Regime's sorry species of liberty: "irregular," "intermittent," "confined," "stunted," "deformed," "disorderly," and "unwholesome" (ii:11, 176–77). It is only in the cavern that is postrevolutionary France, a France hastening to realize those dreams the Economists modeled on a fabulous vision of "the imbecile and barbarous government of China" (iii:3, 213), that the liberty of the Old Regime remains attractive. Tocqueville sees the France of his day possibly saving itself, not by returning to the absurdities of the near or distant past, but by rising above them.

The writing of *The Old Regime and the Revolution* is another contribution by Tocqueville toward that act of national redemption. Needless to say, neither he nor any other individual can bring it to pass. Nor has he any simple remedy to prescribe. In the last analysis, what matters is the character of the people. Those who prize liberty only instrumentally for the externals it brings—ease, comfort, riches—are not destined to keep it long. As for "certain peoples"—those for whom liberty is a good in itself, and the highest good—they feel what "mean souls" can never understand. "Do not ask me to analyze this sublime taste; it is necessary to experience it" (iii:3, 217).

If one believes that such peoples exist, one will be driven to ask whether the French are indeed such a people. To this Tocqueville gives no direct answer. Instead he reminds us, with art and address, that this French people once showed themselves capable of the most astonishing pride, confidence, and vigor. Those qualities propelled them to displays of "audacity to the limit of madness"—and "true grandeur" (iii:2, 208). Tocqueville's study invites such a people, capable of unselfish folly on so heroic a scale, to wonder: Would any human greatness lie beyond their reach if only they ceased to deny themselves? In daring to prove themselves capable, as their forebears were not, of being both free and equal, would they not at last have chosen a goal worthy of themselves?

Tocqueville's last work serves as a kind of coda to his first. The great themes running through *Democracy in America* remained the concerns of his life. Tocqueville traces much of the difference in character and outcome of the American and French revolutions to the social conditions and mores prevailing in those countries on the eve of their upheavals. Looking back at those circumstances he thinks he understands how it was that the one revolution was able to channel ambitions into a civil pursuit of "an ideal but always fugitive perfection"; and, correspondingly, how it was in the other that the memories, feelings, and habits of mind of an overturned aristocratic order served to whip up and sustain the zeal of those who had brought it down. Yet despite these different points of departure, democratic revolutions augur a common end.[9]

As memories of an earlier way of life fade and the preoccupations of a life "spent in eagerly coveting small prizes within reach" grow ever more intense, human greatness is not in prospect. Chances are that small people will think small and cut their dreams to suit their chances. Tocqueville does not preclude the possibility that high ambition might sometime surface in a democratic society. Finding little opposition, such a political figure might take on a singularly "violent and revolutionary character." Yet the larger and more probable danger is that democrats will relax into pettiness. The self-imposed diminution of humankind, abetted by authorities intent on power for themselves and on cozy slumber for the rest, bodes a world dishonorable to the species and fatal to its liberties. Here the custodians of memories of the past might make a difference. In reminding their contemporaries of other ways and earlier aspirations, revolutionary historians also offer the next generation "a higher idea of themselves and of humanity."[10] That rehabilitation of human pride is the first step back from the abyss.

9. Tocqueville, *Democracy in America*, 419–20, 603–7 (vol. 2, pt. 1, chap. 8; pt. 3, chap. 19).
10. Ibid., 604, 606, 607 (vol. 2, pt. 3, chap. 19).

Revival through Recollection

In isolation, the political argumentations of Edmund
Burke, Abraham Lincoln, and Alexis de Tocqueville seem as
distinctive as the political situations in which their speakers
find themselves and the special character of the people they
address and seek to persuade. Like the true politicians they
are, they attend to particulars and then shape the form, style,
and tone of their speech accordingly. In truth, none of them
would ever be mistaken for the other; and yet, notwithstanding these singularities, we find that when we juxtapose their
several productions some strikingly similar qualities come to
sight. We sense that these men are engaged in comparable
efforts.

Recalling the past is the mode all three choose for accom-
plishing an urgent political task. Each invokes a return to
earlier ways as a corrective to contemporary policy. In doing

so they take care to claim nothing for their own authority or on their own behalf; rather, the reverse. For all their words— brilliant, dazzling words at that—these men would have us turn our thoughts away from themselves. If we are to regard them at all, perhaps it should be as cowled figures pointing mutely to some remote object on which we need to fix our minds. By losing themselves in a bygone age, so to speak, they draw attention away from their own will and art. Yet, paradoxically, their acts of seeming self-effacement aim to raise their own generation's sense of human worth and efficacy.

Perhaps there was never a Golden Age, a time of heroes when human beings spoke directly with the gods; but there was the next greatest thing, the "Age of our Revolution." From the perspective of those revolutionaries' descendants— troubled, misled, and rudderless—that earlier generation can appear larger than life. Or is it that the descendants have strangely shrunk? Burke, Lincoln, and Tocqueville will countenance neither conclusion. They reject idolatry and dismay alike, and for much the same reason: those in the grip of either are all too ready to decline responsibility for their collective future. Each of these statesmen understands that there is no hope for his people unless they succeed in breaking through the prevailing habits of mind and action that are being fostered by shortsighted politicians in high places. Each understands that the attainment and preservation of the revolution's promise requires nothing less than a regeneration of national dignity and will.

With a wisdom at once profound and politic, these statesmen grasp the need for major reforms and the concomitant need to conceal innovation from a people all too ready to twist and turn. By draping their reformation in the robes of restoration they do more than legitimize the new and restrain the restless. Tactically these are of course important moves, but these men have more fundamental objectives in view. The rebirth they seek calls for great new efforts, efforts enlisting not only the resources of a masterly rhetoric but all the power and aptness of an argument drawn from a common past. Their manner of speaking invites a people to assert, and to deserve to assert, a sense of national pride. They portray a past worth living up to and give heart to the living generation to claim that legacy as their own by right.

At first glance it might appear odd to suggest that pride is wanting among these of all peoples, with their penchants for dominion and bombast. Nor is it obvious how a fired-up sense of importance can be contained within bearable limits and kept from degenerating into presumptuousness. In each case, I would suggest, a people's enlarged field of vision and deepened sense of indebtedness to the past may both liberate and constrain them. They gain a different perspective from which to take in their present situation and possibilities. If contemplating those great models of theirs is in some sense humbling, it is no less a lesson in generosity; for in acknowledging what they owe to those who precede them, people position themselves in turn to merit the gratitude of those who follow. This renewed sense of dedication and purpose might be said to be the object of these statesmen's political *kalām*.

In each case "our revolution" presents a scene at once terrifying and inspiriting. Great risks are run—indeed, nothing is foreordained—and the revolutionaries' very heads are on the block. At the same time, in staking their all in a cause as large as liberty itself, those revolutionaries show to an astonished world what this English or American or French people can accomplish. What is more, they give hope to other peoples and at least stir them to ask themselves whether they too might be capable of comparable large-hearted exertions. To be sure, none of our statesmen will deny that mixed motives, some of them quite unlovely, prompted their revolutionary heroes to act on their own and others' behalf. This underside of the revolutionary struggle enhances the argument of the latter-day defenders in several respects. It preserves a sense of kinship with forebears whose unqualified apotheosis might otherwise place them beyond the kind of love of which a democratic people is still capable. It serves as well as a caution against utopian expectations; even the greatest, our greatest, were but men. Most importantly, it lays bare the difficult choices confronting every generation as they wrestle with the demands of expedience and the call of principle.

This latter consideration, I am persuaded, is the main reason why Burke, Lincoln, and Tocqueville rehearse their version of their countries' revolutions. In those grand moments of national assertion and definition, a later generation may discover an enactment of what they are all too apt to overlook in the heat and fog generated by small minds struggling for small advantage. By recalling a decisive moment when passion and reason were each called upon to give the other its due, a people can gain a fresh perspective on current preoccupations. It is not that contemporary agitations are trivial—far from it. The problem is rather that the issues of the day are being viewed and treated in so shallow a manner as to deprive them of their deserved depth, resonance, and import. Shortsightedness trivializes principle. For all the rantings of myopic politicians, the implicit weightiness of contemporary controversies and the principled issues embedded therein remain unrecognized and unaddressed. Yet such a turn of events can be afforded by a free self-governing people least of all. A posture of nonchalance would leave them forgetful of who they are, hence exposed and disarmed.

Burke, Lincoln, and Tocqueville labor mightily to counter that oblivion. The defense of the regime of their hopes thereby becomes an invocation of a past, addressed to the present, on behalf of a future generation. This appeal to the living must necessarily tread a narrow and politically slippery path. To inspirit without appearing to be merely hectoring, to embolden without abetting recklessness and impatience, to foster deliberation without forgetting the need for decisive action: within such limits the thoughtful politician works his craft. Not least he must try to persuade his contemporaries that in working for the future they no less serve themselves. Thus it is not merely the rhetorical demand of his immediate urgency and desperation, but a truth, that leads Tocqueville to proclaim:

> This great idea belongs not only to you, and it is not only among the founding ideas (*les idées mères*) of your Revolution, but it lives or dies in your hearts depending upon whether one sees there the birth or rebirth of all the elevated sentiments, all the noble instincts that your Revolution has developed, those noble instincts thanks to which you have done all that you have accomplished that is great in the world and without which—I am not afraid to say it—you will do nothing and you will be nothing.[1]

Unlike that modern conservatism which adamantly opposes theory and, indeed, any reference to a philosophic standard by which even a cherished legacy might be judged, the political *kalām* of these statesmen dares to point—however discreetly—to precisely such a standard. It ennobles one's own not merely by reference to its homebred and prescriptive quality but by quiet allusion to notions of right and perfection that transcend merely national and historic bounds. It would be farfetched to regard these three statesmen as philosophers or even as close readers of Plato's *Laws*. But it is in no way absurd to see in their practical productions a wisdom, clarity, and suppleness that bespeak a philosophic presence in their minds.

In addressing their contemporaries about matters of current dispute, these statesmen see fit to make arguments that point beyond the accidental and contingent, beyond the transient issues of the day. They direct the attention of their contemporaries and successors to human possibilities that any and every people might hold in regard and strive for. By seeking to reform their particular political order with a view

1. Alexis de Tocqueville, "Intervention dans la discussion de la loi sur le régime des esclaves dans les colonies" (30 May 1845), in *Oeuvres complètes*, vol. 3, pt. 1, *Ecrits et discours politiques*, edited by André Jardin (Paris: Gallimard, 1962), 125–26.

to those possibilities, Burke, Lincoln, and Tocqueville act not in the spirit of a conservatism suspicious of philosophic radicalism but as enlightened men trusting in the power of their politic speech to save a people from itself. If that attempt bespeaks a statesman's pride, it also carries with it an implicit compliment to others: a people open to being so addressed may indeed be a people capable of rising yet again to greatness. But like the generation that made the revolution, these successors can only pose, not answer, the recurring question: Does the appearance of greatness in "our revolution" inspire further acts of greatness, or only make comparable efforts seem less needful? Through their deeds the living and the unborn would answer that for themselves.

Index

43–45, 47; *kalām* of, 60–61, 65; Lincoln on, 94, 99, 101, 104, 106, 110n
Jesus, 12n
Junto, 7–8, 33, 34

Kalām, 61–66, 75, 86, 90, 101–2, 123, 131
Kalm, Peter, 24

Lincoln, Abraham, 40, 49, 53, 59, 88–111 passim; on American founders, 49–51, 96, 99–100, 101, 104, 106–10; on slavery, 52, 94, 107–10; *kalām* of, 61, 66, 90, 101–2, 110–11, 129–34; on public sentiment, 90–94, 111; on revolution of 1776, 93, 98–105; on Douglas, 93–94, 100, 102–3, 104, 109–10
Locke, John, 22

Madison, James, 23, 36, 37, 40, 107; on the politics of reason, 32; on education, 47–48
Mason, George, 22
Milton, John, 17
Montesquieu, Charles de Secondat, Baron de, 22, 26, 71
Morris, Robert, 36

"Old Fogy," 51
Ovid, cited, 3

Paine, Thomas, 36
Pauw, Cornelius de, 24
Pendleton, Edmund, 15n
Pettit, John, 93

Plato, 60–61, 66, 133
Price, Richard, 36
Priestley, Joseph, 36
Puritans, 41

Racine, Jean Baptiste, 26
Robespierre, Maximilien de, 36
Rousseau, Jean-Jacques, 71
Rush, Benjamin, 23, 40; on education, 42–43, 44–45

Selden, John, 71
Shaftesbury, Anthony Ashley Cooper, first earl of, 80n
Smith, Adam, 22
Socrates, 12n, 59
Somers, John, 80

Taney, Roger B., 93, 110n
Tocqueville, Alexis de, 25, 33, 36, 59, 91, 112–28 passim; *kalām* of, 61, 66, 114–15, 123–24, 129–34; on Frenchmen of 1789, 118, 123–26, 127
Trenchard, John, 31
Turgot, Anne-Robert Jacques, 30, 37, 38

Vaughan, Benjamin, cited, 18n
Voltaire, 36, 71

Washington, George, 37, 40, 106
Webster, Noah, 44–45
Whitefield, George, 18
William III, 79n
Wilson, James, 45–46

"Young America," 50–51